# PRODUCT HARM
## CRISIS MANAGEMENT

## PAOLA CANE

Printed in the United States of America
First Printing 2019
First Edition 2019

10 9 8 7 6 5 4 3 2 1

*To my beloved children Neri and Lea, without whom this book would have been completed at least two years earlier, or else it would have never been written at all.*

# TABLE OF CONTENTS

# INTRODUCTION

A crisis is considered to be a sudden, unplanned and abrupt negative change in an individual's life on community life or in a company one that affects security and needs short responding time.

Companies are facing an increasing number of crises, often consisting of new threats: a product-harm crisis is a discrete event in which products are found to be defective and, therefore, unsafe or dangerous to at least a part of the customer base.

Product failures occur for many reasons. Whether they are exploding batteries, unlabeled allergens in food, product sabotages, E.coli outbreaks, beetles in infant formulas, product harm crisis presents similarities with many other emergency situations: all of them consist in unpredictable events. This could be due to unknown or undervalued causes, which can significantly alter normal business and compromise the safety of the company, its employees, and customers. Whether the reasons are, customers raise questions, big clients cancel orders, investors get anxious, competitors sense opportunity, and authorities come knocking and products have to be recalled.

However, the term "crisis" has not always had a negative meaning.

Originating from the Greek word κρίσις, it meant "separation" and coming from the verb κρίνω, which precisely means "to separate" it was used in reference to the activity consisting in setting the grain apart from the straw and the chaff. Originally, therefore, the term had a clear agricultural derivation from which it comes the translated meaning of "to choose," also understood as "capacity of discernment" and "decision."

The word "crisis" has thus passed to indicate a purely negative condition that concerns a deterioration, a disturbance, or a crack of a certain status quo. But this negative polarization occurred only in the first half of the Twentieth century, when this re-semantization was strongly linked to the economic sphere, especially following the collapse of the 1929 Wall Street Stock Exchange, so that, the meaning of the term became strictly linked to a sudden and negative economic condition.

Nevertheless, the planning, coordination, and execution of response and recovery strategies to company business crises caused by food poisoning issues, epidemic outbreaks, products sabotage, and the consequent scandals and media crises, remind us of the original meaning of the word crises and bring us to the idea that a crisis always requires a decision-making process and proper actions taken: in few words, the capacity of discernment.

From this ancient meaning it emerges that crises have at least this advantage: they force us to react without delay, making choices and taking decisions.

Product harm crises have been often defined as "a firm's worst nightmare". They can have a very serious aftermath from many points of view: starting from the outbreak consequences on public health, the company's reputation, sell-out, finance, up to putting at risk the survival of the firm itself. The management literature has studied, as well as many case histories had witnessed, a surge in the consequences of product-harm crises for a variety of stakeholders, including consumers, the company itself, its investors, as well as competitors.

Increasing number of recalls, potentially worldwide damages due to globalization had boost the interest in product harm crises, on their impact and on the way they shall be managed.

Product harm crises' impact on markets has been studied from many points of view, becoming a topic of considerable interest to economists, marketers, food technologists, sociologist and media experts.

From a firm's point of view, product harm crisis can lead to very costly procedures and cause sell out market share, and financial losses, together with trade bans and price. Moreover, product recalls can ruin brand equity, spoil a company's reputation, severely affect consumer's loyalty, and damage a firm image as well as the image of the industry in general.

Product harm crises can extend their negative impact to the whole product category as the inadequacy of the production process can be perceived to be an industry-wide problem: some case history show emblematically that product harm crises effect are not limited to the company involved, but can dramatically damage the whole sector, including the competitors that try to take advantage of the ongoing rival's crises.

Hundreds of cases, in different segments - such as health products, food and beverages, vehicles, hygiene and beauty, children's products, computers, household appliances, and electronics- can be taken into consideration. Literature shows that recall affects a firm's value on many fronts, undermining the material, and immaterial company assets.

Many elements can influence the extent of this impact, such as the severity of the outbreak.

Nevertheless the way the company manages the crisis is paramount. In a product failure context, the organization's reaction before this situation is decisive in containing health risks, financial damage and in how consumers and stakeholders will perceive the company and its products.

Experience gives the evidence that the way a firm manages the recall affects its impact: companies able to respond quickly and efficiently (responding immediately to the first alarm, issuing speedy procedures, communicating extensively with media) might suffer fewer damages.

Proactive strategies can attenuate the effects of the crises or even turn it into the opportunity of enhancing the company ethically and positively influencing the consumer's judgment and trust.

Some extra ordinary case histories indicate that a recall may either improve the company's image if it adopts a proactive and socially responsible attitude and is consistent and coherent in its communication and transparent in its relationships with media and consumers.

Still, the implications of recall-related managing strategies may be ambiguous, some times unpredictable or even reflecting countertrend, when the company involved is publicly traded in the stock market.

This is probably because the stock market tends to interpreter proactive strategies as a signal of more severe hazards and great potential financial losses. Given the potential damage resulting from a dangerous product crisis, it is surprising that alongside mere procedures (often reducible to botched manuals compiled solely because their presence reassure auditors and authorities), many industries still pay too little attention to an approach based on a method and still have few and poor plans and procedures for crisis preparation and prevention. Therefore, companies need to know how they should design their product harm crisis management to minimize negative impact.

Certainly, some companies, due to the nature of their products, are more likely to be overwhelmed by a dangerous product crisis. Companies that produce goods closely related to consumer safety and health, are more likely to suffer devastating impacts. Product categories such as pharmaceuticals, medical devices, food and children's products (from infant formulas to toys) have faced the most severe problems.

But, apart from that, no company can consider itself immune to it.

The purpose of this book is to provide a practical approach based on the experience of product harm crisis management. It will be useful to support the industry during a product crises in order to avoid the most classic errors that can undermine speed of reaction, the effectiveness of corrective measures and the company reputation, in one of the most delicate moment for a company life.

If it is true that the organization's reaction before this situation is decisive in how its consumers and stakeholders will perceive the company and its products, it is necessary to assess the fundamental factors to be observed at such times. Leadership, timeliness, responsibility, consistency, lucidity are just some of the vital elements required by a crises scenario.

This book provides a set of recommendations for leaders and crisis managers in the contemporary business environment, considering a huge variety of cases studied, laying out a number of practical advice to avoid the most classic mistakes, successfully manage product harm crises and possibly make us better managers, woman and man.

# 1. POTENTIAL EFFECT OF PRODUCT HARM CRISES

*Every failure is a lesson*

During World War II, USAF had to face many casualties over German skies as many of its aircraft were being shot down. The Air Force researchers tried to reduce aircraft casualties by data analysis: after each mission, the bullet holes on any damaged aircraft landing back home were accurately recorded, looking for vulnerabilities and how to amend them.

Little by little, data began to show a clear pattern: planes were receiving the most bullet holes to the wings and tail. Over and over again, they saw that the bullet holes tended to accumulate along the wings, around the tail gunner, and down the center of the body. The immediate idea was to concentrate the armor where the planes were getting hit the most. The solution to reduce aircraft casualties seemed to be pretty clear: increase armor in wings and tail, as they were obviously the vulnerable areas.

It was the wrongs decision.

Researchers had only looked at bombers who had returned back, but they should have considered the aircrafts that had been shot down. The reason why planes had fewer hits to the engine is that planes that got hit in that area weren't coming back, while hits to the fuselage could be well tolerated.

This story is a crystal example of survivor bias that happens when we only look at the data of those who succeed and exclude those who fail.

Survivor bias is all over, even in product harm crisis management.

A product harm crisis is an expected and sudden event due to a defective, unsafe, or dangerous product that is threatening public health. Product harm crises, sooner or later, give origin to product recalls: a recall is a compulsory procedure, specified by law, of recovering hazardous products from consumers in order to protect and preserve consumer's life, health, integrity, and safety, and avoid material and moral damages.

Literature is rich in case-studies of companies who risked everything, who were predicted to declare bankrupt after a product harm crises, and then succeed to survive and now are still alive and kicking.

We all dwell on success. But looking only at the positive outcomes can cause a false sense of security and preparedness. We tend to be too self-confident and forget that a product harm crisis can have disastrous effects. All too often, unfortunately, the impact of a product harm crisis is compounded because managers have prepared neither themselves nor their collaborators for appropriate responses once tragedy strikes. And crises can strike any company at any time, regardless of company size, where in the world they operate, or even how careful the company is in trying to manage risk.

The grand narratives of product crises history have often been focused on the firms that got their strategies and organizations "right," rather than those that got them wrong, and towards the winners rather than the losers.

Behind each story of success, there are hundreds of instances of failure. Companies that have failed are rarely analyzed, and only a few studies profile the entrepreneurs who went bankrupt after facing a product harm crisis. Among the most longstanding criticisms of business studies is the bias caused towards studying successful firms rather than failures, and the related use of longevity as a major criterion for success.

Few circumstances test a company's reputation, competence, and ability as severely as a product harm crisis. Although crises have a low probability of occurring, they may have severe consequences for a company if not handled properly: they are low-probability, high-impact event that threatens the viability of a firm and is characterized by ambiguity of cause, effect, and means of resolution. For those reasons, product harm crises have been defined as ' the worse firm's nightmare" [Van Heerde et al., 2007].

Their impact on markets has been studied from many points of view, becoming a topic of considerable interest to economists, marketers, food technologists, sociologists, and media experts.

Previous literature has enlightened that recalls can have serious consequences on public health, cause consumers' panic, lead to very costly procedures and cause, clean-up and containment costs, liability costs, sell-out market-share and financial losses, together with trade bans and price fluctuations [Laufer and Coombs, 2006; Rhee and Haunschild, 2006; Siomkos and Kurzbard, 1994; Van Heerde, Helsen and Dekimpe, 2007; Chen et al., 2009] and the need for substantial investments to rebuild a tarnished brand image.

Moreover, recalls can ruin brand equity, spoil a company's reputation [Chen et al., 2009], severely affect consumer's loyalty, damage a firm image as well as the image of the industry in general [Buzby, 2001; Verbeke, 2000].

Some companies had experienced really severe consequences, and in some cases, the survival of the firm itself was at risk. While small recalls, causing little media attention, may go unnoticed, the major product harm crises often result in huge losses, and some companies had experienced such severe consequences that didn't manage to survive.

Therefore, aware of the survivor bias, we will start from those cases, where companies didn't do it, so to keep in mind that if not proper handed a product harm crises can escalate to the most irrecoverable effects.

Takata Corporation was a Japanese automotive parts company that had production facilities on four continents. It was controlling 20% of the airbag market, equipping vehicles of the main carmakers, and the year its founder Juichiro Takada died at 74 in 2011, Forbes magazine listed him as Japan's 29th richest person, worth some $900 million. His airbags and seatbelts had made him wealthy, and his business was thriving.

But this was until a recall ballooned into the biggest car product recall of all times, and led the firm to file for bankruptcy. The first accident linked to a defective device was reported in 2004 in the U.S. when an airbag in a Honda vehicle in Alabama deployed in an unusual way. Consequently, in 2008, Honda Motor Company recalled 4,000 Accords and Civics (2001 model) as Takata airbag inflators were likely to produce excessive internal pressure causing them to rupture and spray metal fragments in the car.

Later in 2009, teen cheerleader Ashley Parham died in a minor accident that occurred in Oklahoma: the airbag in her Honda Accord exploded, shooting metal fragments into her neck and causing her fatal injuries at the presence of her youngest brother. Honda and Takata settle for an undisclosed sum (see ANNEX I for District court of Oklahoma County files) to compensate the family.

Soon after that, on December 24, 2009, Gurjit Rathore died suddenly and tragically in front of her three children after shopping for Christmas present when she was involved in a minor accident driving a Honda Accord. She was killed when her driver's airbag deployed and the airbag inflator, manufactured by Takata, ruptured, resulting in shrapnel passing through the airbag, entering her neck and severing her main blood vessels.

Consequently, Honda expanded the Accord recall in February 2010 and later in December 2011. During the same period, at least 16 deaths and 180 injuries around the world were related to Takata airbag rupture spread of metal fragments, leading Toyota, Honda, Nissan, and Mazda Motor Companies to recall 3.4 million vehicles globally due to possibly defective airbags.

Little by little, the situation appeared more and more dramatic, in 2016 it came up that automakers would have to recall about 42 million vehicles in the USA, with nearly 70 million Takata airbags unsafe or at risk: the unprecedented recall affected roughly 16% of the 260 million vehicles driven on American roads.

After certain airbags that were supposed to have been manufactured properly were also found to be defective, a recall in 2016 expanded to 100 million cars globally. Table 1 resumes the number of airbags repaired in the period 2008-2017 in the USA.

**TABLE 1: AIRBAGS REPAIRED FROM 2008 TO 2017 IN USA BY THE MAJOR CARMAKERS**

| COMPANY | AIRBAGS REPAIRED |
|---|---|
| Honda | 10385975 |
| Fiat Chrysler | 1855890 |
| Toyota | 1802783 |
| Ford | 530836 |
| Subaru | 385596 |
| BMW | 385880 |
| Nissan | 336891 |
| Mazda | 263996 |
| GM | 211861 |
| Mercedes Benz | 12750 |

Source: National Highway Traffic Safety Administration, May 2017

According to the U.S. Justice Department, Takata was already aware in around 2000 that its airbags did not meet the required quality standards, but concealed that knowledge from automakers. Takata internal mails stating that there was no choice but to deliberately doctoring test data had been circulating.

Finally, in January 2017, Takata agreed to plead guilty to wire fraud as a result of its 15-year scheme to falsify information about airbag inflators to make the performance of the airbag inflators appear better than it actually was, including by omitting that, in some instances, inflators ruptured during testing. Even after the inflators began to experience repeated problems in the field, Takata executives continued to withhold the true and accurate inflator test information and data from their customers [United States Department of Justice Criminal Division Fraud Section, 2017]. Too late, Takata agreed to pay $1 billion in criminal penalties, to retain an independent compliance monitor, and to cooperate fully with the department's ongoing investigation. Chart 1 shows the completion recall rate for some major carmakers as of May 26th, 2017.

**CHART 1: COMPLETION RATE OF THE TAKATA AIRBAG RECALL IN USA**

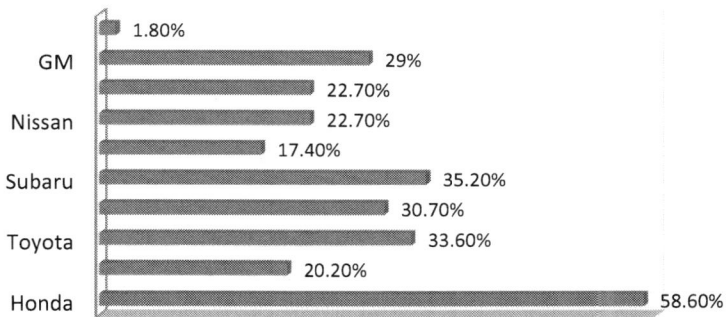

Source: National Highway Traffic Safety Administration, May 2017

The collaboration of the carmakers, the trust of the customers, the credibility of the company was already collapsed and when on June 25th, 2017, Takata finally announced its decision to file for bankruptcy protection, the company had less than two billion yen in cash and deposits and its surviving assets have been sold to its main competitor, a Chinese owned company.

Takata history is surely one of the biggest ever product recall, which reminds us that even the biggest companies can be jeopardized by a dramatically overwhelming impact, and that time does not always heal all wounds.

Takata's is not an isolated lesson.

Above all, let's mention the infamous case of Topps, a historic US maker of frozen hamburgers, that at that time it was considered one of the USA largest manufacturers of frozen patties, it was declared bankrupt just few days after recalling 21.7 million pounds of frozen patties contaminated with E. coli on October 2007.

On September 25th, 2007, Topps Meat Co. recall started out small, involving just a three-day production. But less than a week after, a full year's production was recalled because it came out the company failed to follow its own hazard analysis critical control plan (HACCP) mixing batches of ground beef, with no clean break between lots, spreading the risks of E. coli contamination to the whole annual production and expanding the recall to 21.7 million lbs. of frozen ground beef patties produced between Sept. 25, 2006, and Sept. 25, 2007.

Although Topps has listed $12,000,000 in insurance to cover the claims of the victims of the E. coli outbreak, at least thirty people in eight states had E. coli infections matching the strain found in the Topps patties, but fortunately no death. Punitive damage claims from retail outlets and even from the suppliers of the meat, put the company out of business, with 87 employees losing their jobs.

Even when the consequences of a crisis from a dangerous product do not lead to the bankruptcy of the company, the consequences can be just as dramatic in other, not less important, profiles: just think about the consequences on public health, particularly when the victims are children.

In 1993, another infamous case of contamination of the E. coli outbreak nearly forced the US fast food restaurant chain Jack in the Box out of business. When 732 people were affected by one of the most food poisoning outbreak in American history, this caused the death of four people, all of them children. The company's economic loss was reported to be approximately $160 million in the following 18 months, not considering the costs of hundreds of lawsuits from poisoned customers, that still is nothing compared to the death of four young victims.

On January 12, 1993, a pediatric gastroenterologist notified the Washington State Department of Health of an increase in emergency department visits for bloody diarrhea and the hospitalization of three children with the hemolytic uremic syndrome. The first investigations suggested exposure at Jack In The Box restaurants. Soon after, lab analysis confirmed *E. coli* was isolated from 11 lots of patties in Jack In The Box hamburgers in California, Nevada, and Idaho.

At that time, most Americans had never even heard of E. coli, and even FDA was unprepared to face the outbreak. The outbreak "broke" the weekend of Bill Clinton's first Presidential inauguration, and it was one of the first exigencies that faced the new administration. President Clinton called congressional hearings regarding the safety of the food supply, and the FDA raised recommendations on the internal temperature of cooked hamburgers to 155 degrees Fahrenheit.

Fortunately, product harm crises do not always prove to be fatal to human and business, but even after the less disruptive product harm crises, the product can result less appealing, brand switching among consumers may be higher, marketing mix effectiveness may be reduced and the product under recall may be more vulnerable to competitive actions.

There are still many elements that can influence the extent of a product crises impact to be considered. Apart from the severity of the outbreak, the way a company manages the crisis, its organizational response, and time are some of the most important factors in high and medium extent product harm crises.

It can seem obvious, but worth mentioning, that product harm crisis does not only affects directly to the defected product, but their negative impact can potentially exert influence on the other products of the company [Krysten, 1987]. Moreover, negative implications can also extend to competitors, overwhelming a whole product category, as the inadequacy of the production process can be perceived to be an industry-wide problem [Chen et alt. 2009; Verbeke SEP 2000; Cane 2018]. In this context, it is now worth mentioning the case of E. Coli outbreak occurred in Europe in 2011. The event occurred due to the contamination of organic sprouted seeds as one of the most severe foodborne outbreaks in Europe that resulted in the loss of 53 lives and 857 cases of the hemolytic uremic syndrome [Coombs, 2009].

During the first two weeks of the outbreak, losses for farmers in the fruit & vegetable sector were estimated at least 812 Million € (source: Copa-Cogeca). In addition, a temporary export ban of vegetables to Russia occurred, constituting a loss of 600 Million € for European farmers. The outbreak changed the eating habits of the majority of the population [DG SANCO, 2011], and it had enormous economic consequences, particularly for farmers producing fresh salad ingredients, because European consumers had massively refrained from buying vegetables because of uncertainty on the source and lack of clear recommendations on how to consume veggies safely [DG SANCO, 2011].

Sometimes a crisis can effectively exploit the weaknesses of an entire sector. Let's mention the case 2018 of the Romane Lattuce recall, when a multistate E. coli outbrake was linked to Californian romane lattuce. Both the United States and Canada suddenly registered increasing numbers of people confirmed with infections from E. coli O157:H7, some of them developing kidnew failure. Neither country had reported any confirmed deaths in relation to the outbreak.

Almost immediately E. coli-tainted water used to irrigate the crops was confirmed to be the source of contamination at one California farm, Adams Bros. Family Farms. But soon after FDA declared that "one farm cannot explain the entire outbreak," and even if authorities ware not able to track down other contamination sources, investigations implicated at least 10 distributors and dozens of food manufacturers using romaine lettuce on their preparation.

FDA warned the public and businesses against eating or selling romaine unless they know for sure it is not from previously specified regions of California, but traceability practices prove to be far from being best practices.

Consequently FDA encouraged the entire leafy greens supply chain to adopt traceability best practices, in order to protect the public during a foodborne illness outbreak but the lacks of the traceability system led to a sudden collapse in confidence in the entire sector. Moreover Media advised people to stop eating romaine, and many did.

The financial impact of the recall extended widely. According to Nielsen reports on National Salad Month, during the week that the news broke, romaine dollars sales fell 20%, but also the rest of salad performance was pushed down double digits: iceberg lettuce dollar sales were down 19%, red leaf lettuce dollar sales fell 16% and endive sales dipped 17%. For months prices for romaine lettuce were down 60%.

Extension to the whole category of the negative impact of a product harm crises is typical in the food sector. Food safety reputation (in terms of consumers' confidence and expectation) is strongly correlated with food category. Categories with a stronger safety reputation are typically those that own a certification (organic or designation of origin) or those made by ingredients that are believed to be healthier and essential to human nourishment such as fish, veggies and water. This can easily be a double-edged sword, which can result in a far stronger disapproval and concern when the brand fails to keep their promise of health and quality. People expecting safer and healthier food feel threatened. Previous studies indicated that recall can have much more negative effect on the categories that are considered more trustworthy [Cane, 2018].

During the prolonged out-of-stock situation often associated with a product recall, customers may switch to competing brands, or even decide to quit buying the category. Some case histories show emblematically that product harm crisis effects are not limited to the company involved, but can dramatically damage the whole sector, including those competitors who try to take advantage of the ongoing rival's crises [Mowen, 1981]. In June 1996, when Kraft Foods recalled its two peanut-butter products, due to more than 100 cases of salmonella poisoning, its main competitor Sanitarium took advantage of the crisis by investing in massive advertising campaigns that stated that it had been roasting its own peanuts to avoid foodborne outbreaks. Even if Sanitarium' s market share increased from 15 to 70 percent during the crisis period, the overall demand for peanut-butter went down by almost 30% due to general distrust in the whole segment.

Consumers' interest in product safety issues become the source of increased media scrutiny in recent years, this, often leading to dramatic headlines that represent the major threat to the reputation and equity of brands or companies. Media coverage of product safety issues can be very influential in eroding consumer confidence. Some authors [Borah and Tellis, 2016] define "perverse halo" (or negative spillover) the phenomenon whereby negative impacts on brand image due to product recall extends form a brand name to another. Perverse halo is asymmetric, being stronger from a dominant brand to a less dominant brand than vice versa. Furthermore, these halo effects affect downstream performance metrics such as sales and stock market performance.

Thus, we cannot delude ourselves that negative consequences are exclusively due to media visibility. The increase in the number of high-profile product recalls in recent years highlights the issue of ensuring product safety in global supply chains, and even if a product crisis doesn't fall under the media spotlight, it will be under the retailers' scrutiny, whose reaction can be more immediate and stronger than any other long-term effect as they will immediately assign blame for observed performance.

While consumer reactions in terms of consumer trust, involvement, quality perception, and purchase intention have been widely investigated, retailers' reactions aren't, mostly because of the fact their reaction mainly relates to interruptions of contractual relationships, product delisting, supply interruptions that rarely go under the media spotlight. Nonetheless, however, has experienced such an occurrence knows perfectly that they are definitely "silent but deadly."

Case history and previous literature show that companies able to respond quickly and efficiently (responding immediately to the first alarm, issuing speedy procedures, communicating extensively with media) might suffer fewer damages.

Evidence indicates that a recall may either improve the company's image, if it adopts a socially responsible attitude and it's consistent and coherent in its communication and transparent in its relationships with media and consumers [Mowen, 1980; Siomkos, 1989; Siomkos, 1999; Hammel, 2016; Magno, 2010; Magno, 2012].

That's why product harm crisis management- from the first moments – shall be fast, accurate, responsible, informative, efficient and transparent. An effective recall and proper crises management can gain plaudits from authorities, public and press: successfully handling a crisis is therefore essential.

As we saw, product crises are obviously a risk factor for every company doing business, and the threat of a viral product crisis must be taken seriously. Given the number of parts, processes, suppliers, types of consumers, and product uses encountered, it is probably only a matter of time for any product manufacturer to have one or more of its products recalled [Berman, 1999].

Even the most attentive and virtuous firm cannot completely control the risk that one day, whether due to external or internal causes, it will be subject to a product harm crisis. Some industries are more vulnerable to product harm crises: automotive, food and feed, pharmaceutical, toys are just some of the most exposed sectors, with wide dissemination of cases, bat generally speaking no industry can feed crises immune.

In many cases, preventing crises may be nearly impossible, but having an effective strategy can help a company minimize damage and recover faster.

# 2. DEFINE A STRATEGY

*The essence of strategy is choosing what not to do*

Product harm crises, by definition, take on very different connotations: the types of crises are numerous, varying from 'small-scale organizational issues' to grave crises caused by internal or external factors, such as sabotage and tampering, and may happen to any company at any time.

Despite the fact that many executives believe that their company is relatively immune to crises, no company is totally exempted from a crisis.

Therefore, managers should be effectively-prepared to deal with it, and this preparation may include the ability to choose a suitable product harm crisis strategy.

The basic process that leads to a potential product recall is relatively straightforward, and almost all legal system provide specific and effective tools and procedures to act in response to health threats in case an hazardous food product have been already hesitated for consumption. In the very beginning, the firm receives information from consumers or distribution channel members about the potential hazard of a product. Often, such information comes from consumer complaints directly to either the firm or the distributor, or to the authorities. Whatever is the reason a product is identified as potentially harmful; the firm can decide to act in many different ways.

Previous literature [Siomkos e Kurzbard, 1994] has classified companies' response to crises into four different grades that make up the so-called company response continuum:

- Denial: the company simply denies any responsibility for a defective product, delays investigation on the possible risks and their causes, does not undertake its responsibilities and tries to sweep the issue under the rug;

- Involuntary recall: the company recalls the product only under authority order; this strategy has been defined as 'simple compliance with the minimum legal requirements' [Siomkos, 1989].

- Voluntary recall: the company chooses to recall the product prior to authority intervention in application of the precautionary principle; before a recall becomes inevitable and compulsory, quick responses lead to lower losses in brand reputation than a denial or conservative response [Dawar and Pillutla 2000; Siomkos and Kurzbard 1992]. Delayed recalls, in contrast, can damage the brand's reputation and also increase litigation risk.

- Super effort: the company responds by being socially responsible transparent and proactive. This response may also include the giving of free samples of another product and special discounts. In addition, the company informs customers about the harmful product and how they can be compensated.

At one extreme, choosing the "denial" strategy, firms forsake, or try to forsake any responsibility for the defective product by denying culpability and delaying the recall process.

When external parties cause crises, i.e., the company is a victim of sabotage, or damage is caused by product misuse, a denial response may seem to be justified in pragmatic terms. But even when external parties are responsible, a denial strategy may not work well: consumers tend to judge a denial strategy like a selfish, defensive reaction with a negative impact on the company's image and reputation.

Delaying recognition of the magnitude and urgency of the threat has been the go-to crisis communication method for many professionals in the past decades, but research and case histories show that denial is often the wrong approach, one of the most dangerous enemies of a good crises management.

This is not only especially true if your organization sooner or later will be found guilty, but it's true also in the very first beginning of a harmful event, when it may be necessary to take actions and communicate to the public before having precise information about the origin of the problem. Omissions, delay of communication, of response, ignoring who demands answers are proved to worsen the situation.

In 1985, a number of incidents, injuries and deaths have been related to unintended and sudden acceleration of Audi 5000s model. At the first complaints, the company denied there was a problem, stating incidents were due to drivers mistakes.

On March 1986 Audi was pressured to respond to a recall request made by the Center for Auto Safety to the U.S. National Highway Traffic Safety Administration (NHTSA). Audi delayed its response for months. Then it announced that it would replace the idle stabilization valve and relocate the brake and gas pedals on 132.000 Audi 5000s. However, in its July 1986 recall, instead of performing those tasks properly, Audi installed a gearshift lock that required drivers to depress the brake before shifting into gear. By May 1987,

1700 incidents were recorded and seven dead were officially connected to Audi 5000s defects. The new had devastating effects on the brand: hundreds of consumer lawsuits had been filed, victims constituted a "Audi Victims Network", a class action was initiated, nine of the nation's 409 Audi dealers had dropped the franchise, and many others were dissatisfied, sales were stuck, resale value fall down dramatically not to mention bad publicity and competitors actions to take advantage of the situation.

Soon after the recall, an adverse television report, *60 Minutes,* plunged the knife in and again, reporting unintended acceleration, while the brake pedal was depressed. Subsequent investigation revealed that *60 Minutes* had engineered the vehicle's behavior. Again Audi reacted too late: even when the investigation was debunked, the damage was done.

The cost of the recall to Audi was estimated at $25 million, which is almost the typical costs for automotive recalls of that scale, but these costs are nothing compared to the general consequences of the recall.

Audi sales, which had reached 74,061 in 1985, collapsed to 12,283 in 1991 and remained level for years, with resale values falling dramatically dropped 80 percent over the next five years. It wasn't until 2000 that it regained its peak from 1985. Audi recall had a generational impact: it took more that fifteen years to rebuild a once golden reputation. Before the recall Audi was perceived to be a luxury brand, and after the recall it was nearly to leave the American market.

If sales are an indicator, Audi sell-out performances showed many potential buyers were considering Audi ownership is risky indeed.

The case of Trans World Airways (TWA) flight 800 gives us another eloquent example. Trans World Airlines Flight 800 was a Boeing 747-100 that exploded and crashed into the Atlantic Ocean near New York on July 17, 1996, at about 12 minutes after takeoff. All 230 people on board died. The airplane involved had one of the best safety records in aviation history, with only 1.6 fatal accidents per million departures. Even if in the aftermath of the crash, there was some media speculation that more could have been done to prevent the disaster, despite the lack of obvious prodromal warning signs, the real thing that kept TWA in an unfavorable media spotlight for months was not providing timely information or concrete data about the incident and the victims.

Confirmation of the passenger list took much longer than anticipated, however, and a *New York Times* article reported that four days after the crash, there were only 101 bodies accounted for, and only 46 victims identified. New York City Mayor Rudolph Giuliani fiercely condemned TWA's CEO, Jeffrey H. Erickson, for failing to notify families of victims in a timely manner and reported to the media that Erickson lied to him about the passenger list, which was not released to the press and the authorities for 23 hours after the crash for reasons unknown. Not only Jeffrey H. Erickson, but also the appointed spokesperson for the company ware largely criticized for the way they both handled the crash during the initial and acute phase.

Erickson, who had never handled a major disaster despite his many years in the aviation industry, was in London at the time of the crash and did not address the public until after he returned to New York.

When he came back to the USA, he refused to answer any questions, taking refuge behind a no comment and came across as a bottom-line executive worried more about his company's income than the lives lost on Flight 800.

Following the incident, the media criticized TWA's failure to provide consistent and timely information. Soon after Erickson tried to strengthen the public's positive feelings towards himself and TWA, stating that TWA's primary effort was in providing families support, but again denied TWA's responsibilities: when asked why families were not getting the information that they wanted, Erickson stated that "part of the problem is because there is still so much of [the] airplane under the water", shifting blame from his company to the rescue teams.

Gerald Meyers, a crisis-management professor at Carnegie Mellon University, argued that "[Erickson's] response had been truly lacking. He should have been on the front edge of the company's response and leading the way and showing compassion, and he hasn't been visible". When he was visible to the public, Erickson often came off as a cold and indifferent CEO who was only concerned with his company rather than the lives lost in the crash.

At the other extreme, "super effort" is the proactive strategy of a firm that responds promptly and effectively to consumer complaints, issues speedy voluntary recalls, communicates extensively with consumers and other stakeholders, collaborates with authorities, establish a toll-free telephone hotline for questions and often provides additional compensation beyond the legal requirement. Super effort exhibits primary concern for customers' welfare rather than saving company resources [Siomkos and Shrivastava, 1993].

The firm tries hard to present a responsible image. It recalls the products immediately and compensates the victims. It exhibits primary concern for customers. It informs customers about how to return the defeat product and may offer special discounts and coupons of another product. A firm that takes responsibility and shows concern or sympathy is regarded as more honorable and sympathetic, which leads to more positive reactions.

Although it involves large costs, proactive strategies are often considered the best solution to avoid a loss in consumer loyalty during a recall crisis. In fact, especially in the first phase of a product harm crises, super efforts can actively and concretely contribute to public health protection, playing a decisive role in limiting material damage to consumers and, consequently, to the company. In fact, super effort strategies may lower the company's risk in product liability trial.

For example, Johnson & Johnson's response to Tylenol's product tampering crisis in 1982 made a hero of the firm (International Herald Tribune 2002) and the company's crisis management procedures during the 1982 Tylenol recall are still today, after more than thirty years, a reference model.

Prior to the 1982 Tylenol was the number one pain reliever in the USA market and J&J's single most important profit maker. On September 29 1982, Mary Kellerman a 12-year-old girl woke up complaining of a cold. Her parents of gave her a painkiller, and At 7 a.m. they found the girl dead on the bathroom.

The same day, a 27-year-old postal worker named Adam Janus of Arlington Heights, Illinois, died of what was initially thought to be a massive heart attack.

His brother and sister-in-law, Stanley, 25, and Theresa, 19, were both weak with distress over the unexpected death and each of them took a Tylenol extra-strength capsule from the same bottle Adam had used earlier in the day. Stanley died that very day and Theresa died two days later.

Doctors initially suspected that Mary and Adam died from a stroke, but the deaths of the three family members led to a more sinister diagnosis: they all turned out to be potassium cyanide poisoning: in the next days, a series of deaths were attributed to poisoned Tylenol in the Chicago metropolitan area.

While the blood samples were being tested for cyanide at the Northwest Community Hospital, the fact that victims had all take Tylenol before they died suggested that all the deaths could have been related to the medicine.

McNeil Consumer Products, a subsidiary of Johnson and Johnson and the maker of Extra Strength Tylenol, was immediately alerted to the deaths. J&J began a huge recall of its product and warned doctors, hospitals, and wholesalers of the potential dangers. However, by then, it was too late for three more victims.

Soon after the national news stories on the tragic deaths from the tainted Tylenol, widespread fear swept throughout the country, especially in Chicago and its suburbs. The police drove through the city using loudspeakers to warn citizens about the potential dangers of Tylenol.

Almost immediately, it became clear that the production plant and the medication itself were safe: Food and Drug Administration officials hypothesized sabotage: suspicion fell on James W. Lewis, who in October 1982 sent a letter to the drug manufacturer demanding a million dollars for an end to the poisoning. Arrested and then convicted, Mr. Lewis spent 12 years in federal prison for extortion but was never charged with the Tylenol murders. Nevertheless, investigators were convinced that the killer bought Extra-Strength Tylenol capsules over the counter, injected cyanide into the red half of the capsules, resealed the bottles, and sneaked them back onto the shelves of drug stores.

J&J did the right thing: massive communication was prepared, directed at physicians, hospitals, retailers, and distributors aimed at explaining risks and withdrawal procedures: from 35% to 40% of the total Tylenol line was removed from retailers' shelves. CEO J. Burke became an icon of public responsibility: he was collaborating with the press, showing himself an open and proactive interlocutor. He declared that the firm would spend $100 million to withdraw Tylenol capsules from the market and cover the other expenses arising from the poisoning.

On October 11th, 1982, Jerry Knight wrote in The Herald Tribune, *"Any business executive who has ever stumbled into a public relations ambush ought to appreciate the way Johnson & Johnson is responding to the Tylenol poisonings.*

*Extra Strength Tylenol capsules may not survive in the marketplace, but Johnson & Johnson executives have effectively communicated the message that Tylenol is as much a victim as the people who swallowed cyanide-laced capsules.*

*Though the hysteria and frustration generated by random murder have often obscured the company's actions, Johnson & Johnson has effectively demonstrated how a major business ought to handle a disaster. What J&J executives have done is to communicate the message that the company is candid, contrite, and compassionate, committed to solving the murders and protecting the public.*

*The temptation to disclaim any possible connection between the product and the murders must have been difficult for the manufacturer to resist, yet there is no evidence J&J even considered trying to tough it out. Expressing horror at the deaths, the company moved quickly to trace the lot numbers of the poisoned packages and almost immediately posted a $100,000 reward for the killer. When investigators issued a warning not to take any Tylenol capsules, the manufacturer did not whimper about over-reaction, though surely it might have.*

*Rather than resist, Johnson & Johnson has carefully, one step at a time, escalated its actions to deal with the crisis. First it shut down the Tylenol capsule production line, then it withdrew all capsules from sale. McNeil executives went on ABC's Night Line and the other networks' morning news shows to promise the capsules would not return to the shelves until a tamper-proof package had been perfected.*

*Finally, on Thursday, J&J offered to exchange all Tylenol capsules for Tylenol tablets. More than 22 million bottles of Tylenol capsules are believed to be in consumers' medicine chests and on pharmacists' shelves, almost $80 million worth of the drug at retail prices. There may not be a drop of cyanide in any of those* *bottles, but all of them will be destroyed, the company decided on its own initiative. Replacing the capsules with tablets will cost Johnson and Johnson tens of millions of dollars, a stunning amount even for a popular and profitable drug like Tylenol. Almost $400 million worth of Tylenol was sold last year, more than 40 percent of it in capsule form. Tylenol was the best-selling single product of the $5.4 billion company that is best known for Band-aids and baby products.*

*The company won't talk about its strategy but does acknowledge it has three task forces at work trying to rescue the reputation of Tylenol.*

*It's reasonable to speculate that Johnson & Johnson executives did not decide to swallow the cost of the Tylenol recall simply because they are nice people. Their marketing strategy for Tylenol has been anything but generous. From the day the deaths were linked to the poisoned Tylenol until the recall on Thursday, Johnson & Johnson has succeeded in portraying itself to the public as a company willing to do what's right regardless of cost.*

*Serving the public interest has simultaneously saved the company's reputation. That lesson in public responsibility -- and public relations -- will survive at Johnson & Johnson regardless of what happens to Tylenol."*

The poisoning led to stringent packaging regulations for over-the-counter pharmaceutical drugs, including led to the widespread adoption of tamperproof packaging in food and medical products, providing vital protection for public health.

In 1990, Fortune magazine inserted J. Burke into its National Business Hall of fame for the following reason: *"Few managers of corporate crises have survived an episode of the perfect crime in which their product was the murder weapon and their customers the innocent victims. Indeed, James Burke may be the first CEO ever to have confronted such a horror. He managed it so well that he not only restored Tylenol but he also enhanced the company's reputation"*.

Previous literature and many case history evidence that the ability of companies to react promptly and responsibly to a product harm crisis is fundamental to limit the risk of suffering serious losses and damage to the tangible and intangible assets of the companies involved.

But there is a but: when companies are listed on the stock exchange, the market does not always react by rewarding responsibility. Investors may use interpreter proactive recall strategies differently from consumers; for them, proactivity and responsible strategies are the signals of potential severe financial losses.

The 2019 cases involving again Johnson & Johnson with the opioid crisis and the baby powder voluntary recall give us a sobering demonstration. On August 26th, 2019, J&J was sentenced by the Oklahoma judges to pay a $ 572 million fee for causing the "opioid crisis." The fault of the colossus, ascertained by the court, was having conducted "deceptive and dangerous" marketing campaigns that led doctors to prescribe opioid-based painkillers more than they should, endangering patients' health with tremendously complex public health consequences. Despite the 572-million-dollar fee, in the six hours after the sentence was pronounced, the J&J share price rose continuously. That was because the State of Oklahoma implored the judge to deliver a record $17.2 billion verdict against J&J, but the judge ordered to pay a far smaller fine than expected.

Later in October 2019, J&J announced the voluntary recall in the United States of its baby powder in response to an FDA test indicating the presence of sub-trace levels of chrysotile asbestos contamination (not exceeding 0.00002%) in a single bottle purchased from an online retailer. Despite the low levels reported and recall in full cooperation with the FDA, shares of J&J fell 6%, making it the second worst-performing stock in the Dow Jones Industrial Average. An explanation for this surprising result is that the stock market interprets proactive strategies as a signal of substantial financial losses to the firm. When a firm proactively manages a product recall, the stock market infers that the consequence of the product harm crisis is sufficiently severe that the firm had no choice but to act swiftly to reduce potential financial losses [Chen 2009]. Stockholders fear responsible and proactive strategies are signs of a greater danger: investments always protect themselves.

Whatever strategy a firm embraces, corporate activity during a crisis can be divided into two phases: the phase of the initial response and the phase of reputation recovery. Especially in the first phase, operations may actively and concretely contribute to public health protection, playing a decisive role in limiting material damage to consumers and, consequently, to the company. The better the first phase will be managed, the easier it will be to regain the consumer's trust and the market shares. This leads to another important concept in managing crises: the importance of having the right tools to carry over the operation needed.

# 3. PLANS OR PLANNING
## *He who fails to plan is planning to fail*

areful preparation and planning is a key step to any endeavor. Plans and procedures are an essential part of any organization and provide a roadmap for companies' operations, ensuring compliance with laws and regulations, giving guidance for decision-making and streamlining internal processes. Preparedness is extremely important in any occasion, and it's even more so in time of crises. In conditions of absolute emergency there is no time to plan: in times of crisis it's time to act. Managing a product harm crises or a recall requires coordination, cooperation and quick actions that often need to match urgent needs with scarce resources. It's probably, alas, that a crisis shuts down ordinary operation – if only for a few hours, causing productivity and revenue loss. Without proper preparation, a few hours might tragically stretch out into days, or even weeks: having a plan before the crisis strikes can help minimize downtime.

Hence, many companies use Crisis Management Plans to prepare management paths for them. Usually a Crisis Management Plan contains few fundamental elements that determine the overall structure:

- Crisis management team and contact sheet;

- Stakeholder contact sheet;

- Risk assessment grid;

- Incident report form and notification forms;

- Strategy worksheet; [SEP]

- Media monitoring;

- Post-crisis evaluation [SEP] and recovery intervention;

Some of them are Bible-like six thousands pages manuals that nobody even dares to open. Others are extremely synthetic schemes; the worse of them are the result of copying and pasting standardized models, not customized to the needs and the company profile, prepared only to comply with some certifying body or just because "in case someone will ask, we bury him with a ton of paper".

A Crisis Management Plan could be an effective tool for managing certain aspects and saving time, providing practical information, useful forms to proceed with notifications to competent authorities, but no matter how long and precise it is, a Crisis Management Plan may have limited efficacy.

First of all, despite the number of products affected by recalls is constantly growing, product crises events are still considered peripheric to the core activities of many companies; consequently many plans are ignored until the crisis emerges. No one reads them in advance, no one updates them, no one tests them with simulations. They remain on dusty shelves for years, or saved in the most remote corner of the server. Hence, an emergency plan needs to be a living document that is periodically adapted to changing circumstances.

Given the low probability to many managers and employees of having gained enough experience in dealing crises in previous career experience, the Crisis Plan efficiency is directly correlated to its ability to provide clear instructions to take proper actions without delay. Many plans are often focused on procedures, but they lack on imposing the acquisition of operating routines. Reacting properly under pressure is a pretty rare instinctive skill, and even more rarely, it's paper-based. Plans need to be read and put in practice to gain confidence with protocols and might be tested at least once a year.

There is nothing healthier than simulating emergencies: schools ensure that fire evacuation drills are periodically carried out to get prepared for emergency situations and protect children, teachers, and staff members. When not in actions, military spend a lot of time undergoing training so that their ability to simulate and rehearse with tremendous effectiveness has made the difference between success and failure in recent conflicts. Civil protection exercises are fundamental to teams to react fast and coordinately when disasters occur. But in company's crises training is still rare: nevertheless it will allow team members to familiarize with their roles and responsibilities within the organizational crises response plan and understand the overall emergency management system.

Exercising and training constitute a key task to get ready for a crisis, even through periodic crisis scenario simulations. Training can teach team members how to act coordinately, how to acquire the right automatism, and how to respond promptly even under pressure. Acquiring a method takes time and training: having a manual is not enough.

Some authors [Coombs 2007, Fearn-Banks 2001] noticed how Crises Management Plan can save time during a crisis by pre-assigning some tasks. Pre-assigning tasks presumes there is a designated crisis team as well as team members are aware of their tasks and responsibilities. As unbelievable as it may seem, as the crisis breaks through, at the first convocation of the crisis management team, many members discover for the first time they are designated members of the team, or even when they admit they knew it, they remark that they have never received any formal training or directions.

Nevertheless, plans efficacy is limited by the fact that planning for every contingency is impossible; there is no one-size-fits-all plan for dealing with product crises [S.P. Costello and K Furfari, 2013]. Moreover, being crisis prepared doesn't mean companies to plan for every conceivable disaster. The unpredictable by definition cannot always be foreseen: it is therefore extremely important that crisis management plans provide a methodological approach since only the acquisition of a method can help to face completely unknown situations, operating in conditions of stress and urgency. Crises are no routine.

Many Crises Management Plans are limited to standard procedures, drafting generic declarations of intent, values, and principles that do not suggest a working method, a logical, organizational, and mental structure to manage and resolve the emergency.

Disregarding its limits, having a plan can cause a sense of security and preparedness as if it is a miracle remedy. In case of crises, many managers' expectations about the plan will turn out to be far away from what can be realistically achieved via a crisis management plan and this leads to a widespread sense of impotence and panic.

Given the limitations of a plan, then why do we support the importance of planning? Because planning and preparedness are a different thing from having a plan.

Understanding the distinction between planning and having a plan is very pertinent for every crisis manager, and once again, a military anecdote can help to get the point.

Helmuth Karl Bernhard Graf von Moltke (Parchim, 1800 - Berlin, 1891) was a Prussian general, field marshal, chief of staff of the Prussian army, craftsman of many victories over the Austro-Hungarian Empire and on France. Known as Moltke the Elder, he is considered one of the greatest military strategists in history, particularly for its ability to maneuver large armies in a flexible way, coordinating the movements of the various groups, being able to overcome unexpected situations, concentrating forces in the right moment and at the right point, gaining an overwhelming superiority on the battlefield. After studying for many years rigid, inflexible, and totalizing military theories, that have been proved to be successful until Napoleon, Moltke the Elder had to face some disruptive war innovation that broke into pieces his previous strategic learning. War was no longer about man in tights firing front-loading muskets, new war machines were dominating the battlefield: the invention of the "revolving gun", faster to reload than any other firearm, and the discovery of nitroglycerin and dynamite dramatically increased the complexity of battles. On this scenario Moltke the Elder understood that deterministic plans has become a mere scholar exercise, they were no longer relevant, nor useful. In these circumstances he coined the often quoted saying "no plan survives first contact with the enemy". In his essay "Ueber Strategie" written in 1871, he wrote *only a layman could suppose that the development of a campaign represents the strict application for a prior concept that has been worked out in every detail and followed through to the very end [..] Certainly the commander in chief will keep his great objective continuously in mind, undisturbed by the vicissitudes of events. But the path on which he hopes to reach it can never be firmly established in advance. Throughout the campaign he must make a series of decision on the basis of situations that cannot be foreseen. The successive acts of war are thus premeditated designs, but on the contrary are spontaneous acts guided by military measures. Everything depends on penetrating the uncertainty of situations to evaluate the facts, to clarify the unknown, to make decision rapidly and then to carry them out with strength and constancy"* [Moltke, 1995]. Therefore he designed a new method of directing operations based on as a series of plug-in points that could be fashioned and molded to fit each situation.

He didn't have a plan, but a system, a method, an attitude.

Some decades later, U.S. President Dwight D. Eisenhower (Denison, 1890 — Washington 1969) had a similar approach. His famous saying: "plans are worthless, but planning is everything" (that comes from his speech on November 14, 1957 to the National Defense Executive Reserve Conference in Washington, D.C) [D. Eisenhower ,1957] may seem a paradox. He went on to explain: *"There is a very great distinction because when you are planning for an emergency you must start with this one thing: the very definition of 'emergency' is that it is unexpected, therefore it is not going to happen the way you are planning."* President Eisenhower again remarks that while following the original plan in constantly changing circumstances is often not a good idea, the existence of a guidance tool enables us to produce an almost-optimal strategy [A.F. Garcia Contreras et alt, 2017].

Therefore, a Crisis Management Plan shall be not crafted nor intended as a step-by-step guide to how to manage a crisis. Think of the plan as a reference tool: a crisis management plan is not a device of control or an operative tool that can solve any situation, it's just better equipped to effectively respond to specific incidents, preparing systematically for future contingencies, including major incidents and disasters. The best way to make these guidelines effective is to go through a periodical simulated crisis to see and correct what people actually do step by step.

# 4. TIMELINESS AND ACCURACY

*Crises and deadlocks have at least this advantage:*
*that they force us to react without delay*

S peed and timeliness are crucial elements in dealing with crisis scenarios: fast shall be the collection and updating of data, fast shall the transmission of the flow of information, fast the decisions and the corrective actions that follow, fast the communication.

Small companies are generally faster and more able to react quickly. This depends, in part, on the greater flexibility of smaller corporate structures, but also on greater sensitivity to pre-alarm signs that large companies often ignore, even for years.

Between December 2017 and February 2018 Lactalis, one of the major dairy French companies (just behind Danone and Nestlé), was forced to proceed with one of the biggest recalls of its kind, pulling out of the market thousands of tons of Salmonella tainted baby formula across more than 80 countries.

In the beginning, the company ordered the recall of 16.000 boxes of the production of one of its factories over fears of possible contamination with salmonella, but it was just the tip of the iceberg.

Day by day, the situation appeared to be more critical than initially thought. Information received from the health authorities, as well as the results of initial investigations, led the group to issue a second recall, this time of all products manufactured in the Craon factory, since February 15, 2017, using a specific drying tower that was the source of the contamination. The second recall involved 720 batches sold in France, India, and China. The scale of the entire operation was impressive: more than 12 million boxed of infant formula affected, removed from the shelves all around the world, and destroyed. The recall spread at last to 620 batches of Lactalis products for both internal UE market and export. Soon after the first recall, new salmonella cases were reported, and the firm appeared unable to say whether the contaminated milk was still on the market, consumed, or in stock. Also the French health authority was indeed under fire for the way they handled the crisis.

In the exhausting days of the last recall, the Company was accused of hiding the previous discovery of salmonella. In fact, despite previous salmonella episodes involving the same plant, the firm had taken the decision not to inform the authorities that internal tests had discovered salmonella on a broom and on the tiles of a dehydration tower at the company's Craon factory in August 2017. This was a decision hard to defend, especially when it emerged that the salmonella was the same strain of the one found in the Lactalis 2005 outbreak. Suspects that ten years of production could have been tainted arose. The missteps along the way exposed corporate lapses and regulatory gaps that allowed contaminated baby products to make their way into the market, for years and years before any proper action was taken.

Lactalis recall and his impact on infant health and could have been mitigated if the firm was able to read the warning signs and take appropriate corrective actions. Ignoring data, signals, test results are not going to solve anything: if you postpone the moment the crises break trough, it might be even more dramatic.

The first hours of any crisis, often called the "Golden Hours", are the most delicate moments, when most organizations fail, mostly because they underestimate the need of giving rapid and clear response, nor they understand the potential media attention they are willing to get, or even because they do not know they are in a crises.

In the very first hours of crisis management, it is, therefore, appropriate for the crisis team to undertake the following activities:

- Maintain self and situational control
- Take proper action to limit or control the problem.
- Communicate with those affected, including victims and families.
- Communicate with employees, authorities, community, customers, clients, suppliers, and shareholders.
- Communicate with the media and other channels of external communications, in a coordinated way.

Considering that crisis scenarios are, by definition, changeable, speed and timeliness are crucial elements in addressing a crisis management strategy: quick shall be the collection and updating of data, the information flow, the decisions, and the corrective actions that follow.

Giving out precise and quick information is very important, especially when a crisis deals with public safety: consumers and stakeholders need to know how to avoid risks and what actions are needed [Fearn-Banks 2007].

Communication must be fast, accurate, direct, and transparent... and, even if it seems obvious, the communication shall be formally correct.

It may sound incredible, but many recall communication are full of misspellings, copy and paste mistakes, an erroneous indication of lots, or are lacking the data needed to contact the company. It can be hard to believe, but I have collected recall messages with any kind of error, including mistyping of the CEO's name.

Working tidily, completely, precisely, is a good habit that may remind you of elementary schools and handwriting exercise books, but in the middle of a recall is much more than that: it is a legal obligation.

Sloppiness is a bad habit that denotes a lack of professionality. Moreover, the way we communicate is a sign that denotes respect for consumers, authorities, and stakeholders and even for the eventual victims of our harmful product. But, if this is not enough to give you a spurt of pride and tidiness, it can also lead to fees.

A crisis is a circumstance that requires attention: any words matter.

Business operators may inform their customers about the non-compliance found in their product in an effective and accurate manner: clear shall be the reason for the market withdrawal, clear shall be the way to avoid risks, and achieve a high level of health protection.

If I need to write down crises affair guidance or recall messages, I work better if I find a few minutes on my own. Certainly, I keep my problem and my objective continuously in mind, but I need to work and write undisturbed. I recall to my mind some previous works of mine, or I check out my archive for some text that I found to be especially effective.

I write down a first draft, which will normally be reduced by at least two thirds, eliminating everything that is not essential, relevant, and informative. Writing more has to be the same meaning of scaffolding a building: it's a temporary structure used to support my work to aid in the construction, indispensable in the creation phase, but doomed to go away when the work is finished. Then I double-checked misspelling, the lot number, and all the when, where, who, and what.

Speed does not mean doing things badly: in the midst of chaos and excitement of a product harm crises, even if it is Christmas Eve and our family is waiting for us in front of the fireplace, you must have the discipline to write carefully, choose each word, double-check and correct, before giving out any statement.

By communicating, it is necessary to keep in mind that what we say is addressed to a wide range of interlocutors, including potential victims.

Communication efforts, therefore, must not only concern what is communicated, but also in what way, using a tone consistent with the situation and the interlocutors.

Too many communications relating recalls are so wrong that they need further integration or even to be retracted within a few hours.

Although speed is important, so too is accuracy. The example of the Galaxy Note 7 crisis shows us an exemplary case of how, in order to communicate in a timely manner, the accuracy of the information provided has been neglected for a month.

In August 2016, Samsung launched the Galaxy Note 7, working around the clock and rushing impossible deadlines since the iPhone 7's launch date was set in September.

On August 24th, the first report of a Note 7 explosion emerged in South Korea, and consequently, Samsung declared that shipments of Note 7s to South Korean carriers were to be delayed. Nevertheless, on September the 1st, Samsung started Galaxy Note 7 sales in China. On Sept. 2nd Samsung announced a global recall of 2.5 million Note 7 phones, citing faulty batteries, hiding that the risk due to faulty batteries that overheated and exploded was really severe. In that "golden hours," Samsung aggressively told the media its goal was a 100% recall: the company sent text messages and emails to communicate the recall. Tim Baxter, CEO, and president of Samsung Electronics America, Inc., proudly called it the first digital recall. But the first recall in the United States was launched without required coordination with the Consumer Product Safety Commission, and wasn't effective, especially because it was initially presented to customers as a sort of "exchange program."

Less than a fourth night later, a Florida consumer sued Samsung for burns from a Note 7 explosion. Consequently, the U.S. Consumer Product Safety Commission formally announced the recall of about 1 million Note 7 phones. Again the recall was not effective, and in late October, U.S. authorities intervened, expanding the recall to 1.9 million Note 7 devices. At the end of October, Samsung discontinued the product.

Following the entire chronology of the major developments related to Samsung's recall of the Note 7s since the launch until the end of October (ANNEX II) shows many contradictions: the data provided by the company were often confusing, unclear and the choices made by the firm were incoherent. But the most impressive fact, apart from the number of press releases, recall messages, decisions taken and activities are undertaken without a logic, was that company had suddenly been overwhelmed by panic as if catapulted into an infernal group.

As a result, the recall cost Samsung something like $5.3 billion.

For an organization that prides itself on rapid action and execution, Samsung was relatively quick to find a fix when problems first emerged with the Note 7, but the fix was problematic itself. Moreover, they gave too much information too soon at the onset of the crisis and had an embarrassing amount of different retractions.

Sometimes, in the middle of a harmful event, it may be necessary to communicate to the public even before having precise information. Ignoring who demands answers will only worsen the situation: journalists, consumers, and social networks would end up filling the void of information autonomously.

The inability to provide rapid and punctual information can worsen exposure to risk, aggravate the scenario, and irreparably compromise public health and consumer safety, and with their safety, that of the company.

But sometimes you do not have precise information.

In such cases, the company must provide attention to pressing interlocutors, implementing a "Buy-Time Communication", that is, able to take time, to reassure that attention is high, reduce the tension, avoiding a flourishing of inferences, demonstrating the commitment towards the values dear to the interlocutors, as in the following example:

## IMAGE 1: EXAMPLE OF BUY-TIME COMMUNICATION

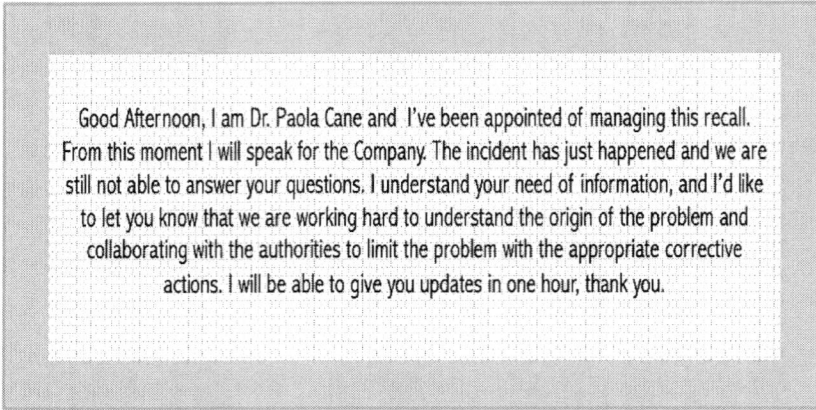

> Good Afternoon, I am Dr. Paola Cane and I've been appointed of managing this recall. From this moment I will speak for the Company. The incident has just happened and we are still not able to answer your questions. I understand your need of information, and I'd like to let you know that we are working hard to understand the origin of the problem and collaborating with the authorities to limit the problem with the appropriate corrective actions. I will be able to give you updates in one hour, thank you.

One of the most important things you can tell reporters and audiences is that you care. That you understand their need for information, so your "Buy-Time Statement" might be concentrated on the need to reassure that the attention is high, to reduce any tension, to avoid a flowering of illations, to demonstrate your commitment and commit about a rapid update.

Your crises team will take advantage of every time you buy: for them, it will be easier to work: for many employees and managers, it will be hard to maintain high performance if under high emotional pressure for extended periods. Some time to work without the pressure of the media will be useful to decrease stress levels and help re-gaining rational behavior and concentration.

Moreover, the media and the consumers will understand that information and action don't occur in a vacuum and that the company is coordinating with the appropriate authorities.

A buy time communication would have been better than the solution embraced by Perrier when they start giving out messages about the benzene contamination without having a clue of what the reason was.

Before the 1990 recall, Perrier mineral water was not only a market leader, it was an icon, and its trademark had almost become a generic word for "water" like Coca Cola, Jacuzzi or Kleenex are used to indicate the entire product category.

At that time, chemistry laboratories around the world often used Perrier water to dilute their solutions. Perrier water, in fact, was considered perfectly suited to the purpose because of its purity, and it was more convenient than producing distilled or purified water inside the laboratory.

It was January 19th, 1990, when a biologist at the Mecklenburg County Environmental Protection Department in Charlotte, N.C., noticed unusual traces of benzene in his sample. According to The Economist, everything came out on a simple routine test that turned on unusual results. The lab team first thought it had to be an equipment failure. Then, after spending some days in testing and retesting every tool, every utensil, every machinery, they realized that the Perrier water they used to dilute the test solution contained some minor quantities of benzene.

Perrier North America immediately reacted with a recall, announcing that the problem was due to a cleaning fluid uses on a bottling plant in North America. The problem seemed to be limited to the USA and Canada, no victim has been wounded, but the truth was that Perrier had really no idea of the source of benzene contamination.

The Company disseminated inconsistent stories over the media, hoping the dust would settle, totally forgetting to communicate with national and overseas distributors, clients and wholesalers (that found out about the benzene scandal by the media). Only after official investigation and many days later, the company had to retract its own previous statements and disclose that actual cause was a filter at the natural spring in France. Only in Europe, the benzene contamination resulted in the recall of 160,000,000 bottles. Market share dropped form leadership position to 8% in the USA, consumers, retailers, and wholesalers were all let down by the way the firm had handled the situation.

This led to an irrecoverable loss of customer loyalty and quality perceptions, and the brand never re-established to the pre-recall sales level. Residual damage in retail and ho-re-ca still persist nowadays, even after the re-branding attempts, with a label bearing the expression "Nouvelle Production."

A crisis is a very delicate situation where timeliness and accuracy shall be correctly balanced.

Despite the necessary readiness to analyze the situation, take corrective action, and communicate, it is necessary to avoid the risk of making hasty decisions based on incomplete or inaccurate information or even inadequate and conflicting information on which long-term effects may depend.

# 5. LEADERSHIP AND TEAMWORKING

*It is in times of crisis that real leaders emerge*

Crises management is not easy. The manager of a company hit by a crisis is not a train conductor who drives the company on tracks, but it's a modern captain of a ship that sails in the "perfect storm." Still, there's a few a leader who can do it alone.

The ability to do the right thing at the right time, under severe time and psychological pressure, are both extraordinary rare and difficult. Crises are complex scenarios that require a set of coordinated efforts to understand the situation, exert control over the event, and take proper actions to reduce negative consequences. Crises demand swift and effective decision-making and a well organized coordinate operative structure that turns decisions into proper actions.

During crises, companies need leaders, and leaders do need a good crisis management team.

The leader remains the most important individual: he is exposed to the media and social networks, to the judgment of the shareholders, and above all, he is exposed to legal responsibilities, which he cannot escape.

Driving a company that faces a dangerous product crisis is a complex activity that requires competence, readiness, concentration, awareness, ability to make decisions, speed and linearity of reasoning, but also integrity, intellectual honesty, and courage.

What are the factors that enable the manager to make the right decision under such critical conditions? The decision literature has identified numerous cognitive mechanisms that appear to guide successful managers toward effective decisions [Dawes, 1979; Hogarth, 1980; Klein, 1983]. However, in critical decision situations, leaders experience tons of both cognitive, intuitive, and emotional processes that interact instantaneously [Kleinmuntz, 1990]. The complexity of the context requires, in summary, the maximum commitment both in the rational area and in the emotional one.

Effective leaders who enable their organizations to recover from a crisis exhibit a complex set of competencies and soft skills in any phase of a crisis, from signal detection, to damage control and containment, from business recovery, to reflection and learning.

## IMAGE 2: LEADERSHIP SKILLS

| COMPETENCY | A leader shall possess adequate knowledge so that he can take into account all relevant information and consider each of the most probable outcomes. |
|---|---|
| LUCIDITY | Intended as clearness of thought, and ability to maintain self-control in order to choose between right and wrong. |
| DECISION MAKING | The ability to identify and choose between two or more possible solutions |
| LISTENING | Leaders should establish a steady flow of communication between themselves and their team members, either through an open-door policy or making themselves regularly available to discuss issues and concerns with employees. |
| MINDFULNESS | Complete awareness of the situation |
| INFLUENTIAL | Able to gain consensus without searching for it, without apparent exertion of force or direct exercise of command |
| COURAGE | Mental or moral strength to venture, persevere and withstand danger, fear, or difficulty. |
| INTEGRITY | Fair and straightforward, with clear moral values. |
| RESPONSIBILITY | Willing to undertake his responsibilities and to stand off his choices |

Image 2 summarizes some of the skills that make the ideal profile of a leader.

The indications provided are too often far from reality. I have seen so far too many managers that do not behave like leaders should do, and, if on one hand crises enhances leadership, unfortunately, on the other hand it is the pretty perfect occasion to spot bad leadership.

Bad leadership is often characterized by typical signs, in the presence of which crisis management could be easily compromised.

Leaders prone to a sense of invulnerability are very dangerous: a sense of invulnerability [sep]promotes excessive optimism and encourages decisions of very high risk. [sep] Very often, this happens when the leader has already faced extreme ease previous crises and are too comfortable taking a gamble: they might think they are a sort of Arabian phoenix, always able to rise from its own ashes. Taking on too much risk can have dire consequences.

A leader that displays an inviolate belief in himself can be as fatal as a leader in total panic. Anxiety, fear, and stress are human emotional reactions that up to a point can be considered absolutely natural. They are not a sign of weakness until they do not take the upper hand nor guide the leader's response.

Even worse, some leaders tend to present the crisis as the result of a series of unfortunate coincidences that could have happened to any of its competitors, trying to spread the message that the crisis is the mirror of a widespread nonconformity that regards the entire competitive landscape. These leaders often tend to stereotype authorities, consumers, and stakeholders as enemies, as evil entities trying to attempt his and the company's survival.

Some leaders apply direct pressure to any member who questions their arguments. Also in time of crises, in the middle of the perfect storm, a leader shall be ready for receiving advice, discussing and listening to his employees feedback and indications, knowing that there is always someone that knows something he doesn't know.

When a leader displays one or more of these symptoms in a crisis situation, it will generally produce poor quality decisions that are likely to bring on a disaster for the organization.

Although the importance of the leader, a step toward successful outcomes from a crisis event is to develop a good crisis management team working together with specific skills and responsibilities, clearly assigned and understood.

The outcomes of an effective team exceed the sum of the isolated individual contributions of its members; moreover, teamwork helps to increase skills and points of view and facilitates access to information on which decisions are based.

Dealing with crisis requires experiences, capacities and tools that in many cases lacks in managers, as they haven't been involved in any critical issue occurred in the past: as we already saw in the previous chapters, when a crisis strikes conditions are not favorable for training: that's why crisis management team shall be better composed by experienced senior levels.

The composition of a crisis communications team may vary depending on the size of the operation, but keep these three roles in mind: operations, communications, and subject matter expertise.

Other personnel should be staffed on an as-needed basis; this may include Environmental Health and Safety, Engineering, Information Technology, Purchasing, Supply and Distribution, and from time to time, also outside resources that could fill gaps in the team. But be aware that adding too many team members may actually hinder team productivity overall. To ensure efficiency, the perfect number of persons in a crisis team is from five to ten.

Small teams are much more effective: individual effort decreases as the team size increases, and team members will have relatively higher engagement, moreover, in Smaller teams, individuals better share the decisions and responsibilities that follow.

It is appropriate for the crisis management team to be composed of individuals capable of working under pressure, processing a large amount of information, with the ability to concentrate, pay attention, understand, and self-control.

During crises, individuals are under great stress, important decisions must be made within a short time, and stress and panic can affect the quality of the decision process.

It is not uncommon that in times of emergency, managers report a sense of loss of control and stability that often narrows the cognitive processes, no secret that also, for this reason, crisis management represents one of the most complexes of real-world situations.

# 6. OPERATE AND COMMUNICATE

*Managing a product harm crisis is extremely complex because it requires extraordinary efforts on many fronts*

On the one hand, it is necessary to carry on all the activities that help to understand the problem, including lab analysis, tests, and inspections. Then a crisis requires actions to reduce or mitigate risks, to carry out an efficient recall campaign, and to implement a fast reverse logistics. All of this, possibly without losing business continuity, even if the execution of the necessary crisis response often overlaps with the routinary business activities that are necessary for the continuity of operations.

On the other hand, it is necessary to deal with communication. Crisis communication has been defined as "dialogue between the organization and its public prior to, during, and after the negative occurrence" [Magno et alt., 2010]. In the last decades, the media had an increasing appetite for product harm crises [Kumar and Budin, 2006], often exaggerating the matter or even distorting the fact. The public needs to be informed and look for a trusted and consistent source of information, but in absence, anyone can fill the void, especially in the era of the Internet. For stakeholders, consumers, clients, and authorities, the unknown is often worse than the truth; speculation fills the void in the absence of direct and official communication. If this is the scenario, the impact of a product harm crisis can be really exacerbated.

Whether it happens because firms are overwhelmed by the many operational needs, or because they underestimate the importance of communication, or perhaps because they hope to go unnoticed, many companies still neglect or mishandle the communication during a crisis.

In this frame, the majority of communication is out of the control of the company in focus: media set the agenda in terms of contents and coverage, media raise questions, media convoy messages.

Therefore, it is imperative that firms deliberately and coordinately communicate also to reduce negative media scrutiny during the crisis, and to reduce the risk that, without even engaging communications before media overwhelms you.

On August 23, 2008, the Canadian Maple Leaf Foods plant occurred in case of listeriosis contamination that quickly turned into a serious public health problem. More than 20 people died in connection to the Maple Leaf Foods listeriosis outbreak. Many more fell ill. It was one of the worst cases of food contamination in Canadian history.

Immediately, the company issued a widespread recall of 23 luncheon meats, deli trays, and sandwiches to contain the crisis. A week later, Maple Leaf upgraded the recall of 23 to all 220 products manufactured in the plant, which has been shut down. The crises was so severe had the potential to severely damage, or possibly even stop their businesses, but Maple Leaf survived, and today is still a leading food processing company committed to delivering quality food products to consumers around the world, with incredible performance, that in 2018 registered 3,496 million Canadian dollars sales with 9,9% Adjusted EBIDTA.

One of the reasons that contributed to the successful crisis management was that besides having carried out the activities necessary for an effective recall and to contain the food born outbreak, the company has been highly visible since the crisis hit, investing many efforts in leading the communication flow. Maple Leaf Foods' response was voluntary, consistent, capable, committed, and passionate. The firm's CEO, Michael McCain, almost immediately held press conferences where he stated, "Tragically, our products have been linked to illness and loss of life. To those people who are ill, and to the families who have lost loved ones, I offer my deepest and sincerest sympathies. Words cannot begin to express our sadness for their pain. This week our best efforts delivering the highest quality, safe food have failed us. For that, we are deeply sorry. We know this has shaken consumer confidence in us. Our actions will continue to be guided by putting their interest first".

Communication during crisis shall be trustworthy and credible, transparent and reassuring, and should not only contain facts and information, including what is being done and what is going to be done, but it might show caring, compassion, and empathy to create public goodwill and maintain a positive reputation for the organization.

While the company is exposed to the media and social networks, to the judgment of members and all stakeholders, communicating requires a solid and organized message map, that displays the right information and the master message public needs to hear, understand and remember.

Developing public affair guidance and message maps are paramount for responding in an ordinate, consistent, unambiguous way.

First of all, it is important to identify a communication leader that shall be in charge of managing the communication process. Once the communication leader has been designated, all messages relating to the crisis must be drawn up according to his/her guidelines.

The second important step is to identify key stakeholders: consumers, authorities, retailers, investors. Effective communication shall be crafted, keeping in mind who it is addressed to, including potential victims, and shall be focused on the needs of the parties that could be or actually are affected by the situation.

The third step is to develop a complete list of specific concerns for each important stakeholder group. Ask yourself what they will want to know. Prepare a list of uncomfortable, thorny questions. Make up your mind on the top worst questions you could be asked and get ready to answer.

Then develop the master message. Answer to each question addressing top of mind issues, with supporting facts for each statement: do not make an empty intent declaration, they would sound hypocritical. Declaring your concern is not enough. Nor that you are doing everything in your power. Your declarations must be based on facts; please do not invent, don't be intentionally ambiguous, do not make promises that you already know you can't keep. Credibility is your currency. And, please, don't forget to test the accuracy of the technical information you are giving out with subject matter experts to ensure consistency and credibility to your declaration. Subject matter experts can tell if you hold the scrutiny, you will be subjected to.

Once you are ready, deliver the message. Messages can be released through a variety of means, especially today that we are in the Internet era. If you wish or you need to face the cameras, do it by a trained spokesperson. If you do not have one, remember that public talking, especially if under pressure, might need a careful rehearsal. Prepare the message in various forms. Send it to all suppliers, customers in order to ensure that the master message is transmitted in a coherent, coordinated, unambiguous manner. Give precise instructions to those who have contact with the public: provide customer care employees with public affairs guidance to follow.

I will never get tired of saying that all messages shall be coordinated. Unfortunately, there is always someone who releases anapprouved messages, not in line with the overall communication, there is always someone who speaks with stakeholders without being authorized, seeking the famous fifteen minutes of fame. Ironically these are not workers and employees, but very often managers who have been cut off from the crisis team and need, by personal drive, to show the world they are always in charge, and their role is not weakened. Very often, only for vanity, these individuals desire to show that they have access to confidential information. They will damage the company, the entire emergency management process, and in the long run, will damage their own corporate position. These events must be treated severely: crisis communication needs compactness; there is no room for individual opportunism and expediency.

Special attention must be paid to media monitoring. What was once a literal cut-and-paste job – where employees scoured newspapers and for mentions, cut out the articles, and pasted them into physical clipbooks – is now a much more advanced practice, that it uses machine learning, sophisticated algorithms, powerful processors or even the easy google alert tools. Review media, conduct regular searches through Internet search sites for keywords, monitor blogs, social media is important. Social networks do not forgive mistakes and must be kept under constant control: socials can trigger users' anger, attack the company's reputation, and rapidly disseminate information on its behavior.

To monitor social media may, therefore, be a useful capability from a crisis management perspective, both for detecting new or emergent crises, as well as for getting a better situation awareness of how people react to a particular crisis [Johansson et alt, 2012].

# 7. THE RECOVERY PHASE
## *Land as soon as possible*

I've been married to a fighter pilot of the Air Force for almost fourteen years. There isn't a single word to describe what being a pilot's wife is like: it can be truly scary, unpredictable, from time to time unsustainable, mostly bittersweet, for sure it is a non-stop learning experience. At that time, I was still in my youngest and most light-hearted years, far from being a product harm crises fixer, when he gave me a piece of advice that I've been turning over in my mind ever since.

To face any aircraft emergency (and even daily life ones), he had a mantra that for sure has been ingrained into his young pilot's mind while going through the initial phase of pilot training. A four-step process that outlines the proper response to any aircraft emergency, composed this mantra:

"Maintain aircraft control, analyze the situation, take the proper actions and land as soon as possible."

Effective crisis management requires the same four basic elements. We might think comprehensively about product harm crisis management: it is not all about maintaining control over the situation, understanding the causes, responding quickly, while keeping their organizations running: a crisis is not over until we get our business back to the normality.

Landing as soon as possible is a priority, no matter where, since conditions may get worsening, the weather may deteriorate, or other factors can bring sudden additional complications. Too few remember that the goal of crisis management is to land safely as soon as possible, but there is no reason to keep flying with a broken wing and a burning engine.

If we neglect the last phase, when the worst of the crises looks to be over, when the dust begins to settle, the aftershocks might be more devastating and costly than the initial crisis as the implications of a product-harm crisis can go beyond the immediate sales and market-share loss.

If crisis management is "a reactive approach whose purpose is to limit the damage" [Eccles et alt, 2009], it is not over until we get out feet on the ground.

That's why crisis recovery planning should be a part of any strategic planning process. Unfortunately, the recovery phase is too often neglected: even the most sophisticated companies have only a fuzzy idea of what it means, and the existing literature lacks generalizable knowledge on this point.

Depending on the severity of the event, realignment of operations, reorganization of corporate objectives, reassessment of the company's reputation, and regain the brands' pre-crisis loyalty, consumers' trust and sell-out levels might require a long time.

Recovery might seem superfluous for easy product recalls, those that might be considered a quick peanut operation, those that go unnoticed in the media, those that apparently "nothing has happened," but still, this might be a mistake.

Even in better circumstances, it is important to continue monitoring the situation, to learn the lesson, and to put in place appropriate measures to avoid reoccurrence.

Technical recovery is sought through organizational and technological process improvements even if too many case histories show us that few efforts have been made to eliminate the original causes of a product harm crisis.

Economic recovery is sought through compensation to victims.

Business recovery is pursued through financial and product market changes and settlement of damage claims.

Social recovery requires the reintegration of victims into social systems and the normalization of social relations [Quarantelli, 1978].

Sales and image recovery may require extra marketing investment: the idea that after a crisis, advertising investment, effectiveness will remain the same as before is naïve. Required investments may be much higher.

At last, land as soon as possible might also be intended metaphorically like to need to put both feet on the ground has a sensible and practical attitude towards the crisis and its consequences.

Assuming publicly the responsibility for what happened, showing regret for the victims together with the willingness to proceed in a different direction and do change the company's behavior, it's in many cases the best and most honorable way to land s soon as possible.

Anyone who has experienced crisis management consulting or mentoring knows that this is not easy. Admitting mistakes publicly can be difficult and even painful, and many company leaders are scared that public apologies will deprive them of their power and leadership.

In addition, some leaders tend to believe that the public assumption of responsibility entails a clear admission of guilt under the criminal profile. So, they tend to avoid apologizing and proving responsible, as they are afraid of compromising their own position. This is a false problem. Although the assessment of legal responsibilities in a criminal proceeding is a complex process, it must be emphasized that in many legal systems, the reparative and responsible behavior after the infringement might not merely reduce the punishment, but can remove the punishment in toto. In many legal systems, active repentance is a means to extinguish criminal liability for an offense that has already been committed. A growing number of justice institutions, alongside legal regimes based on individual accountability for the crimes committed and commensurate punishment, may provide a positive legal meaning to the public admission of responsibility and apology, together with proper actions to solve the problem and compensate the victims. Moreover, in many circumstances, apologies and admitting mistakes can help rebuilt the relationship with authorities, customers, and consumers. So, apologies and public responsibilities admission can be a door opener towards restorative justice and a proper crisis recovery.

Crisis management history presents some remarkable structured recovery strategies that include an apology. When crafted properly, an apology isn't a liability: it's an asset that can attenuate the effects of the crises or even turn it into the opportunity of enhancing the company ethically and positively influencing consumer's judgment and trust.

Among the most interesting cases, it is worth mentioning the famous Toyota case due to a massive car recall in Japan, Europe and in the USA in response to break defect that caused fatal crashes from 2006 to 2009.

In dealing with public questions about its product reliability, Toyota has countered many critics as, for years, after the first defective cars have been detected, the carmaker hadn't shown any real effort in determining the potential causes of the unitended acceleration in its vehicles. The Japanese company at the beginning of the crisis understimate the problem and

argued that the cause of the accidents was due to driver error or pedal entrapment.

In August 2009 Mark Saylor and three members of his family had just picked up a rented Lexus to go to the soccer game between the University of Southern California and the University of San Diego, when they have been all killed in a terrible crush. Chris Lastrella, riding in the back seat, was able to call 911 while the car was speeding over 125 miles per hour and was on the phone until the fatal crash ended his life. In the emergency call, whose recording were made public, he is heard saying: "We're in a Lexus... and we're going north on 125 and our accelerator is stuck... there's no brakes... we're approaching the intersection... Hold on... hold on and pray... pray."

When the frantic 911 call was made public, America was under shock, the community had plenty of unanswered questions and media attention was intense. The tragedy renewed the government scrutiny on safety problems of Toyota cars.

Millions of Toyota cars had been recalled worldwide, but in the first phase of the recall, Toyota Company has been strongly criticized for its slow response to the crisis. Finding out what was going wrong was troublesome; the carmaker proceeded by trial and errors, and many competitors deliberately took advantage of the situation, causing sales loss and increasing pressure over the Japanese carmaker. One day after Toyota's announced sales suspension;

General Motors began offering a US$1,000 cash rebate targeted toward Toyota owners. By February 1, 2010, Ford, Chrysler, and Hyundai were offering similar incentives.

As of January 2010, 34 deaths were alleged due to the problem, but according to USA Today, the number of victims could be much higher.

It was on February 24, 2010, that Akio Toyoda, the grandson of the company's founder Kiichiro Toyoda, appeared before Congress in Washington, D.C. to testify on the 34 deaths that – up to that point – US authorities had been investigating with a view to a causal link with defects in Toyota and Lexus cars.

Akio Toyota wrote personally his apology stating. *"I love cars"* he started" *"as much as anyone, and I love Toyota as much as anyone. I'm here with my Toyota family of dealers, team members and friends. I take the most pleasure in offering vehicles that our customers loves and I know that 200.000 Toyota dealers and suppliers in America fee the same way. However, in the past few months our costumers of Toyota's vehicle and I take full responsibility for that. Today I would like to explain to the American people as well as our customers around the world how seriously Toyota takes the quality and safety of its vehicles. I would like to focus my comments t on three topics: Toyota basic philosophy, regarding quality controls, the cause of the recall and how we will manage quality control going forward. First, I myself as well as Toyota I'm not perfect. There are times we find defects and in such situations we always stop, trying to understand the problem and make changes to improve further in the name of the company, and its long standing tradition and pride. We never run away from our problems, or pretend we don't notice them. By making continuous improvement we aim to continue offering even better products for society. That is a core value we have kept close to our hearts since the founding days of the company"*.

"*At Toyota we believe*" he continued, "*the key to making quality products is to develop quality people. Each employee things about what he or she should do to make improvement and by doing so, he makes eve better cars. We have been actively engaged in developing people who share and can execute on this core value. It has been over 50 years since we began selling in this great country, and over 25 years since we started production here. And in the process, we have been able to share this core value with the 200,000 people at Toyota operations, dealers, and suppliers in this country. That is what I am most proud of.*"

"*Second, I would like to discuss what caused the recall issues we are facing now. Toyota has, for the past few years, been expanding its business rapidly. Quite frankly, I fear the pace at which we have grown may have been too quick. I'd like to point out here that Toyota's priority has traditionally been the follow: first safety, second quality and third volume. These priorities became confused, and we are not able to stop, think and make improvements as much as we were able before, and our basic stance to listen to customers' voices, to make better products has weakened somewhat. We pursued growth over the speed at which we were able to develop our people and our organization, and we should sincerely be mindful of that. I regret that this has resulted in the safety issues described in the recalls we face today, and I am deeply sorry for any accidents that Toyota drivers have experienced. Especially I would like to extend the condolences from the deepest part of my heart to the Saylor family for the accident in San Diego, and I will do anything in my power to ensure that such a tragedy never happen again*".

"*Since last June, when I first took office, I have personally placed the highest priority on improving quality over quantity, and I have shared that direction with our stakeholders. As you well know, I am the grandson of the founder, and all the Toyota vehicles bear my name*" he almost shouted, raising its tone, in an uncommon way for a Japanese manager. "*For me, when the cars are damaged, it is as though I am as well. I, more than anyone, wish for Toyota's cars to be safe, and for our customers to feel safe when they use our vehicles. Under my leadership, I would like to reaffirm our values of placing safety and quality the highest on our list of priorities, which we have held to firmly from the time we were founded. I will also strive to devise a system in which we can surely execute what we value. Third, I would like to discuss how we plan to manage quality control as we go forward. Up to now, any decisions on conducting recalls have been made by the Customer Quality Engineering Division at Toyota Motor Corporation in Japan. This division confirms whether there are technical problems and makes a decision on the necessity of a recall. However, reflecting on the issues today, what we lacked was the customers' perspective. To make improvements on this, we will make the following changes to the recall decision-making process. When recall decisions are made, a step will be added in the process to ensure that management will make a responsible decision from the perspective of "customer safety first." To do that, we will devise a system in which customers' voices around the world will reach our management in a timely manner, and also a system in which each region will be able to make decisions as necessary. Further, we will form a quality advisory group composed of respected outside experts from North America and around the world to ensure that we do not make a misguided decision. Finally, we will invest heavily in quality in the US, through the establishment of an Automotive Center of Quality Excellence, the introduction of a new position – Product Safety Executive, and the sharing of more information and responsibility within the company for product quality decisions, including defects and recalls.*

*Even more importantly, I will ensure that members of the management team actually drive the cars, and that they check for themselves where the problem lies as well as its severity. I myself am a trained test driver. As a professional, I am able to check on problems in a car, and can understand how severe the safety concern is in a car. I drove the vehicles in the accelerator pedal recall as well as the Prius, comparing the vehicles before and after the remedy in various environmental settings. I believe that only by examining the problems on-site, can one make decisions from the customer perspective. One cannot rely on reports or data in a meeting room. Through the measures I have just discussed, and with whatever results we obtain from the investigations we are conducting in cooperation with NHTSA, I intend to further improve on the quality of Toyota vehicles and fulfil our principle of putting the customer first."*

*"My name is on every car."* He ended up, showing a pretty uncommon emotivism for a Japanese man *"You have my personal commitment that Toyota will work vigorously and unceasingly to restore the trust of our customers. Thank you."*

To understand the tenor of these declarations, we cannot disregard the cultural context in which they occurred, and the importance that apologies assume in Japanese culture, where chief executives routinely make public apologies if their company is in crisis.

Immediately after his speech, Mr. Toyoda's apology was under scrutiny. Opinions about it differ widely amongst media and observers.

However, it is useful to point out that, while assuming responsibility for what happened, the Toyota president managed to distance himself from the conduct that led to the recall and to show the willingness to proceed in a different direction, listing a set of activities to be carried out and committing personally. He publicly admitted that the recall was the undesirable side effect of too quick company growth that was struggling to emerge in the international market, retaining distance from the mistakes that led to the recall, showing sincere regret and willing to change.

A successful apology can turn a dramatic experience into a positive one, an upset customer into a loyal one, and a bad reputation into a great one.

Crisis management is the entire set of activities aimed at removing the causes that generated the crises at containing damages, at solving the problem and, although many believe that the management of the crisis should be aimed at the rapid restoration of the status quo, I believe that the recovery phase shall be possibly aimed at achieving a better situation than the status quo ante. Going back to the status quo ante, in fact, means, in many cases getting back to the same risks. Overcoming a crisis necessarily requires a change, and that will possibly make us be better companies, managers, men, and women.

Crises have another advantage, they remind us that is never too late to do the right thing.

# ANNEX I

*Lawsuit Complaint In Takata Recall*

CJ09 7411 -
Dixon

IN THE DISTRICT COURT OF OKLAHOMA COUNTY
STATE OF OKLAHOMA

FILED IN THE DISTRICT COURT
OKLAHOMA COUNTY, OKLA.

AUG 6 2009

PATRICIA PRESLEY, COURT CLERK

by _____
DEPUTY

MELTON PARHAM, individually and as )
custodial parent, guardian and next friend of )
MELTON PARHAM, JR., )
)
Plaintiff, )
)
v. )  Case No.:  **CJ -2009-7411 .**
)
AMERICAN HONDA MOTOR CO., INC., )
HONDA MOTOR CO., LTD., HONDA OF )
AMERICA MFG., INC., HONDA R&D CO., )
LTD., HONDA R&D AMERICAS, INC.; )
HONDA NORTH AMERICA, INC.; )
TAKATA CORPORATION; TAKATA SEAT )
BELTS INC.; TAKATA RESTRAINT )
SYSTEMS INC.; TAKATA-PETRI INC.; TK- )
TAITO L.L.C.; AND TK HOLDINGS INC. )
)
Defendants.

## PETITION

COMES NOW the plaintiff, Melton Parham, individually and as custodial parent, guardian

and next friend of Melton Parham, Jr., a minor child, and for their cause of action against the

Defendants allege and state as follows:

1.    Plaintiff is the custodial parent and guardian of the said minor child, Melton Parham,

Jr., and brings this action for and on behalf of Melton Parham, Jr., as the said minor

child's next friend.

2.    On May 27, 2009, the minor child was riding as a passenger in an automobile that

-1-

PLAINTIFF'S
EXHIBIT
_m_

was being driven by his sister, Ashley Nicole Parham.

3. While thus riding in the automobile, the automobile was involved in a minor accident.

4. The accident occurred in Oklahoma County, Oklahoma.

5. As a result of a manufacturing defect in a component of the automobile, Melton Parham, Jr.'s sister sustained a fatal injury during the accident.

6. Melton Parham, Jr., observed the injuries to, and the death of, his sister, Ashley Nicole Parham, at the time of and during the immediate aftermath of the automobile accident.

7. As a result thereof, the minor child sustained and suffered personal injuries and damages for emotional distress

8. Melton Parham, Jr. has thereby been damaged in an amount in excess of $10,000.00.

WHEREFORE, premises considered, the plaintiff, Melton Parham, individually and as custodial parent, guardian and next friend of Melton Parham, Jr. prays judgment in his favor on behalf of the said minor child for an amount in excess of $10,000.00 against the defendants, American Honda Motor Co., Inc., Honda Motor Co., Ltd., Honda of America Mfg., Inc., Honda R&D Co., Ltd., Honda R&D Americas, Inc.; Honda North America, Inc.; Takata Corporation; Takata Seat Belts Inc.; Takata Restraint Systems Inc.; Takata-Petri Inc.; TK-Taito L.L.C.; and TK Holdings Inc.

-2-

Respectfully submitted,

Randy P. Conner   OBA No. 12948
Randy P. Conner, a Professional Corporation
2601 Northwest Expressway
601 Oil Center West
Oklahoma City, Oklahoma 73112

Ph.:    405.235.2100
Fax:    405.848.2029
**ATTORNEYS FOR PLAINTIFF**

**ATTORNEY LIEN CLAIMED**

C:\Work Docs\Podany Hendd\Hour Settlement Petition.frx

3

-3-

IN THE DISTRICT COURT OF OKLAHOMA COUNTY
STATE OF OKLAHOMA

MELTON PARHAM, individually and as
custodial parent, guardian and next friend of
MELTON PARHAM, JR.,

     Plaintiff,

v.

AMERICAN HONDA MOTOR CO., INC.,
HONDA MOTOR CO., LTD., HONDA OF
AMERICA MFG., INC., HONDA R&D CO.,
LTD., HONDA R&D AMERICAS, INC.;
HONDA NORTH AMERICA, INC.;
TAKATA CORPORATION; TAKATA SEAT
BELTS INC.; TAKATA RESTRAINT
SYSTEMS INC.; TAKATA-PETRI INC.; TK-
TAITO L.L.C.; AND TK HOLDINGS INC.

     Defendants.

Case No.: CJ-2009-7411

FILED IN THE DISTRICT COURT
OKLAHOMA COUNTY, OKLA.

AUG – 7 2009

PATRICIA PRESLEY, COURT CLERK
by _____
     DEPUTY

## ANSWER

  COME NOW the defendants, American Honda Motor Co., Inc., Honda Motor Co., Ltd.,

Honda of America Mfg., Inc., Honda R&D Co., Ltd., Honda R&D Americas, Inc.; Honda North

America, Inc.; Takata Corporation; Takata Seat Belts Inc.; Takata Restraint Systems Inc.;

Takata-Petri Inc.; TK-Taito L.L.C.; and TK Holdings, Inc., and for their answer to the plaintiff's

Petition on file herein, allege and state:

### ADMISSIONS AND DENIALS

1.  These answering defendants admit the allegations contained in paragraph 1 of the
plaintiff's Petition.

2.  These answering defendants admit the allegations contained in paragraph 2 of the

plaintiff's Petition.

3. These answering defendants admit the allegations contained in paragraph 3 of the plaintiff's Petition.

4. These answering defendants admit the allegations contained in paragraph 4 of the plaintiff's Petition.

5. This answering defendant specifically deny the allegations contained in paragraph 5 of the plaintiff's Petition

6. These answering defendants are without sufficient knowledge or information to form a belief as to the veracity of the allegations contained in paragraph 6 of the plaintiff's Petition and, therefore, deny same, demanding strict proof thereof.

7. These answering defendants are without sufficient knowledge or information to form a belief as to the veracity of the allegations contained in paragraph 7 of the plaintiff's Petition and, therefore, deny same, demanding strict proof thereof.

8. These answering defendants are without sufficient knowledge or information to form a belief as to the veracity of the allegations contained in paragraph 8 of the plaintiff's Petition and, therefore, deny same, demanding strict proof thereof

WHEREFORE, the defendants, American Honda Motor Co., Inc., Honda Motor Co., Ltd., Honda of America Mfg., Inc., Honda R&D Co., Ltd., Honda R&D Americas, Inc.; Honda

North America, Inc.; Takata Corporation; Takata Seat Belts Inc.; Takata Restraint Systems Inc.; Takata-Petri Inc.; TK-Taito L.L.C. ; and TK Holdings Inc., pray for judgment in their favor and against the plaintiff, Melton Parham, in both his individual capacity and in his capacity as custodial parent, guardian and next friend of Milton Parham, Jr., together with their cost of this defense and such other relief as the court may deem just and proper.

Respectfully submitted,

Gary M. Chubbuck   OBA No. 1682
Michael D. Duncan     OBA NO. 11601
FENTON FENTON SMITH RENEAU & MOON
211 North Robinson Ave., Suite 800 N.
Oklahoma City, Oklahoma 73102

Ph.:     405.235.4671
Fax.:   405.235.5247

## CERTIFICATE OF SERVICE

I hereby certify that on this 7th day of August, 2009, I served a true and correct copy of the above and forgoing Answer by United States Mail, Postage Prepaid to plaintiff's counsel of record.

Gary M. Chubbuck/Michael D. Duncan

North America, Inc.; Takata Corporation; Takata Seat Belts Inc.; Takata Restraint Systems Inc.; Takata-Petri Inc.; TK-Taito L.L.C. ; and TK Holdings Inc., pray for judgment in their favor and against the plaintiff, Melton Parham, in both his individual capacity and in his capacity as custodial parent, guardian and next friend of Milton Parham, Jr., together with their cost of this defense and such other relief as the court may deem just and proper.

Respectfully submitted,

Gary M. Chubbuck   OBA No. 1682
Michael D. Duncan     OBA NO. 11601
FENTON FENTON SMITH RENEAU & MOON
211 North Robinson Ave., Suite 800 N.
Oklahoma City, Oklahoma 73102

Ph.:     405.235.4671
Fax.:    405.235.5247

## CERTIFICATE OF SERVICE

I hereby certify that on this 7th day of August, 2009, I served a true and correct copy of the above and forgoing Answer by United States Mail, Postage Prepaid to plaintiff's counsel of record.

Gary M. Chubbuck/Michael D. Duncan

6.      That the attorney for the Plaintiff, Randy P. Conner, is entitled to attorney's fees, costs and expenses in the sum of $_____Ø_____ for his representation of the Plaintiff herein, which sum is to be paid from the Settlement Amount paid by said defendants to the Plaintiff herein.

7.      That the Settlement Amount referred to in paragraph 3 above is deemed to be fair, just and in the best interest of the minor child, Melton Parham, Jr., and is entered into by the parties of their own free will, being fully represented by counsel and after being made fully aware of the circumstances and consequences.

8.      That Plaintiff, Melton Parham, individually and as custodial parent, guardian, and next friend of the minor child, Melton Parham, Jr., is aware that said minor child has a right to a jury trial and said minor child has a right to await reaching the age of majority and up to one (1) year thereafter before bringing this action but, by entering into this settlement, has affirmatively agreed to waive said rights.

IT IS THEREFORE ORDERED ADJUDGED AND DECREED that the Joint Application for Court Approval of Settlement and for Entry of Judgment should be, and the same is hereby, GRANTED; this Court hereby approves the terms of the settlement agreement as set out herein, and further hereby enters Judgment in favor of the plaintiff, Melton Parham, individually and as custodial parent, guardian, and next friend of the minor child, Melton Parham, Jr., and against the defendants, American Honda Motor Co., Inc., Honda Motor Co., Ltd., Honda of America Mfg., Inc., Honda R&D Co., Ltd., Honda R&D Americas, Inc.; Honda North America, Inc.; Takata Corporation; Takata Seat Belts Inc.; Takata Restraint Systems Inc.;

-3-

Takata-Petri Inc.; TK-Taito L.L.C.; and TK Holdings Inc., in the amount of ▓▓▓▓▓▓▓▓
▓▓▓▓▓▓▓▓▓

IT IS SO ORDERED this ___7th___ day of __August__, 2009.

_____
JUDGE OF THE DISTRICT COURT

Approved as to form:

_____
Randy P. Conner   OBA No. 12948
Randy P. Conner, a Professional Corporation
2601 Northwest Expressway
601 Oil Center West
Oklahoma City, Oklahoma 73112
Ph.:    405.235.2100
Fax:    405.848.2029
**ATTORNEYS FOR PLAINTIFF**


_____
Gary M. Chubbuck    OBA No. 1682
Michael D. Duncan OBA No. 11601
FENTON, FENTON, SMITH,
   RENEAU & MOON
One Leadership Square - Suite 800 N
211 North Robinson
Oklahoma City, Oklahoma  73102-7106
Ph.:    405/235-4671
Fax.:   405/235-5247
**ATTORNEY FOR DEFENDANTS**

-4-

# ANNEX II

*Timeline Of The Toyota Recall Crisis*

## 2000

Toyota launched program known as "Construction of Cost Competitiveness for the 21st Century" with the aim of cutting costs of 180 key car parts by 30 percent, saving nearly $10 billion by 2005.

## March 2004

Private Insurer State Farm notified NHTSA of a worrying trend in claims of unintended acceleration in 2002 and 2003 model year Lexus ES300s and Toyota Camrys.

## December 31, 2004

Toyota vehicles accounted for about 20 percent of all unintended acceleration complaints filed with NHTSA in 2004, up from 4 percent in 2000.

## August 2005

NHTSA began a review of concerns about the electronic throttle and uncontrollable acceleration on 2002-05 model year Camry, Solara and Lexus ES models. The investigation was closed in January 2006 without a defect finding.

## September 2006

NHTSA opened an investigation of 2002 to 2006 model year Camrys and Solaras based on complaints of short duration acceleration without pressing the accelerator. The investigation ended without a finding of a defect.

## March 23, 2007

Toyota began investigation of whether floor mats may be jamming accelerators based on five complaints from owners of 2007 Lexus ES 350 cars.

## March 29, 2007

NHTSA opened preliminary investigation about all weather floor mats jamming accelerators.

## July 26, 2007

In San Jose, Camry crashed into another car, killing the driver of the second car, possibly linked to accelerator problems. NHTSA determined that the San Jose crash was caused by the entrapment of the accelerator pedal by all-weather floor mats, and informs Toyota that a recall was required.

## September 13, 2007

NHTSA determined that the San Jose crash was caused by the entrapment of the accelerator pedal by all-weather floor mats, and informs Toyota that a recall is required.

## September 26, 2007

NHTSA opened preliminary investigation about all weather floor mats jamming accelerators.

## December, 2007

Toyota's U.S. sales for 2007 hit 2.6 million units. It has displaced Ford Motor Co as No. 2 in the U.S. market and is on the cusp of unseating General Motors Co as No. 1 on a global basis.

## April 19, 2008

A 2005 Camry, a model not covered by a recall related to pedals, accelerated out of control and crashes into a tree. The crash was investigated as a possible example of problems with the electronic system that controls the throttle and engine speed. Toyota denied there is a problem with the electronic systems.

## June 2008

After years of complaints about acceleration problems, Toyota concluded that the accelerator pedal feeling could change under certain conditions, but that this is a driving issue not a safety issue.

## April 27, 2009

Toyota engineers in Europe sent reports of sticking accelerator problems in Galway, Ireland to Toyota engineers in Los Angeles.

## June 2009

Akio Toyoda, 53, grandson of Toyota's founder, is named president, replacing Watanabe, 67. Yoshi Inaba is called out of retirement to head Toyota's U.S. operations.

## July 2009

In a confidential presentation listing legislative and regulatory "wins," Toyota estimates it saved $100 million by negotiating with regulators to limit a previous recall to 2007 Camry and Lexus ES models for sudden acceleration.

## August 28, 2009

Saylor family died in the crash of a Lexus ES 350 after the car accelerates out of control.

## September 10, 2009

Public release of the 911 audio and transcript from the August 28 crash.

## September 29, 2009

Toyota announces recall of 3.8 million U.S. vehicles because floor mat problems could cause accelerator to stick. Toyota excludes a "vehicle-based cause" for the problem. NHTSA advises owners to remove the floor mats.

## November 2, 2010

Toyota announces a voluntary recall of floor mats, and claims that NHTSA officials had found no other defect, a statement that NHTSA says is incorrect.

## November 25, 2009

Under a recall order covering Camry, Tundra, Avalon, Tacoma, Prius, and Lexus models, Toyota announces more measures aimed at preventing the floor mat from causing the accelerator to stick.

## December 28, 2009

In New Jersey, an Avalon speeds out of control. The driver manages to drive the car to the dealer.

## January 16, 2010

Toyota USA executive urges his colleagues to admit the company has mechanical problems with accelerator pedals.

## January 19, 2010

At a meeting in Washington including Inaba and U.S. sales chief Jim Lentz, NHTSA asks Toyota to take prompt action. Hours later Toyota tells NHTSA it will issue a recall.

## January 21, 2010

Toyota announces recall of 2.3 million vehicles — including RAV4, Corolla, Camry, Avalon, Sequoia, Tundra, Matrix, Highlander, and the Pontiac Vibe

— to fix a problem that could cause accelerator pedals to stick even without the presence of floor mats, though Toyota does not have a solution.

## January 25

NHTSA tells Toyota it is must stop selling vehicles that have acknowledged defects even if it does not have a remedy.

## January 26, 2010

Toyota announces temporary suspension of sales in North America of eight models of vehicles including the Corolla and Camry as it works to fix problems.

## January 27, 2010

Toyota widens the recall by 1.1 million vehicles, expanding the recalls to Europe and China, but has not determined the models and numbers of cars affected.

## January 28, 2010

Toyota meets with NHTSA to review its pedal fix. NHTSA says it has no objections to the fix. But objections to the fix raised on the press.

## February 1, 2010

Toyota announced a repair to fix accelerator pedals by installing a steel reinforcement bar in the pedal assemblies of 2.3 million vehicles in the U.S. Toyota will provide replacement pedals to more than five million buyers whose cars were recalled over floor mats.

## February 2, 2010

Toyota lost market share as sales fall while GM and Ford gain. Ford, GM, and Chrysler offed sales incentives to Toyota owners.

## February 3, 2010

U.S. Transportation Secretary Ray LaHood warned Americans not to drive recalled cars, but later said this was a misstatement and advises drivers to take their vehicles to the dealer.

## February 4, 2010

Toyota acknowledged a flaw in the Prius hybrid's antilock braking system, and safety regulators announce opening of an investigation.

## February 5, 2010

Toyota President and CEO Akio Toyoda promises to enhance quality control.

## February 9, 2010

Toyota announces a worldwide recall of about 437,000 Prius and other hybrid vehicles to fix a problem in the braking system.

## February 17, 2010

Toyota President and CEO Akio Toyoda announced steps to restore trust including installation of new brake override systems and faster disclosure of defects.

## February 22, 2010

U.S. congressmen said that Toyota relied on a flawed study in dismissing the notion that computer issues could be a at fault for sticking accelerators, and that Toyota then made misleading statements.

## February 25, 2010

Toyota President and CEO spoke at a U.S. House hearing, apologizes, and takes personal responsibility.

## March 2, 2010

U.S. Transportation Secretary Ray LaHood said the Obama administration may recommend that automakers install brake override systems.

## March 4, 2010

Federal safety regulators opened investigation of cases of unintended acceleration in Toyotas that were already repaired.

## April 5, 2010

U.S. Department of Transportation seek $16.4 million fine against Toyota.

## April 13, 2010

Lexus suspended sales of the 2010 Lexus GX 460 after Consumer Reports warns buyers of a dangerous handling problem.

## May 18, 2010

Toyota payed a $16.4 million fine to settle allegations by U.S. regulators that the company was too slow to recall cars with gas pedal problems.

## May 21, 2010

Toyota recalled about 3,800 Lexus LS sedans in the U.S. to fix a problem with the steering system, after a similar recall in Japan.

## July 2, 2010

Toyota recalled 270,000 Lexus GS, IS, and LS vehicles worldwide, including 138,000 in the U.S., to fix engine stalling problems.

## July 5, 2010

Toyota recalled 270,000 Crown and Lexus models worldwide for valve springs with potential production issue.

## August 28, 2010

Toyota recalled approximately 1.13 million Corolla and Corolla Matrrix cars Engine Control Modules (ECM) that may have been improperly manufactured.

## February 22, 2011

Toyota recalled an additional 2.17 million vehicles for gas pedals that become trapped on floor hardware.

Sources: Owles and McDermon, Daniel, 2010; MSNBC, 2010; Reuters, 2011

# ANNEX III

*Timeline Of The Samsung Galaxy Note 7 Recall Crisis*

## August 2, 2016

Samsung unveils the Galaxy Note 7 at a New York media event. The initial response is good and expectations high. It's seen as Samsung's big rival to the upcoming iPhone 7.

## August 19, 2016

Samsung starts Galaxy Note 7 sales in 10 markets including United States and South Korea.

## August 24, 2016

Report of a Note 7 explosion surfaces in South Korea.

## August 31, 2016

Samsung delays shipments of Note 7s to South Korean carriers

## September 1, 2016

Samsung starts Galaxy Note 7 sales in China

## September 2, 2016

Samsung announces global recall of 2.5 million Note 7 phones, citing faulty batteries. The company offers to either refund or replace the device.

## September 8, 2016

U.S. Federal Aviation Administration advises passengers to not turn on or charge Note 7 smartphones aboard aircraft or stow them in plane cargo.

## September 9, 2016

U.S. Consumer Product Safety Commission urges Galaxy Note 7 users to stop using their phone.

**September 15, 2016**

U.S. Consumer Product Safety Commission formally announces recall of about 1 million Note 7 phones.

**September 16, 2016**

Florida man sues Samsung for burns from Note 7 explosion. Samsung says to resume Note 7 sales in South Korea on Sept. 28.

**September 19, 2016**

Samsung says a Note 7 phone a China user claims caught on fire was caused by external heating. Samsung starts Note 7 exchange program in SouthKorea.

**September 22, 2016**

South Korea orders extra battery safety measures for Note 7 phones.

**September 25, 2016**

Samsung delays South Korea re-start of Note 7 sales by 3 days

**September 29, 2016**

Samsung says more than 1 million people globally now using Note 7s with safe battery.

**October 1, 2016**

Samsung resumes selling new Note 7s in South Korea.

In the US, the replacement of phone is in full swing.

**October 6, 2016**

A Southwest Airlines plane in the United States evacuated due to smoke from a Note 7 device on board.

## October 9, 2016

AT&T, T-Mobile say they have halted issuing new Galaxy Note 7 smartphones due to safety concerns

## October 10, 2016

Samsung says it is adjusting Note 7 shipments for inspections, quality control due to more phones catching fire.

## October 11, 2016

Samsung permanently halts sales and production of Note 7 smartphones and asks customers to stop using the phones as it investigates reports of fires in new devices.

## October 13, 2016

U.S. regulator expands Note 7 recall to 1.9 million devices, including all replacement devices. Oct. 12 - Samsung slashes its third-quarter profit guidance by a third to 5.2 trillion won ($4.63 billion) from an earlier estimate of 7.8 trillion won, reflecting earnings impact from the Note 7 recall and discontinuation.

## October 18, 2016

Three Note 7 users in the United States file for a class action lawsuit against Samsung Electronics' U.S. unit. Oct. 14 - Samsung says it expects a operating profit hit of around $3 billion for Q4 2016, Q1 2017 combined due to the Note 7's discontinuation.

# BIOGRAPHY

Appel, B., Bol G., Greiner M., Lahrssen-Wiederholt, M., Gross S., Hiller P., Lindtner O., 2012, *EHEC outbreak 2011: an investigation of the outbreak along the food chain*, p. 154. Available at: http://www.bfr. bund.de/cm/350/ehec-outbreak-2011-investigation-of-the-outbreak-along- the-food-chain.pdf. Accessed 12 June 2012.

Baker, G. F. (2001). Race and reputation: Restoring image beyond the crisis. In R.L. Heath (Ed.), *Handbook of public relations*, (pp. 513–520). Thousand Oaks: Sage Publications.

BBC News, Galaxy Note 7: Timeline of Samsung's phones woes https://www.bbc.com/news/technology-37615496

Berman, B. (1999), *Planning for the Inevitable Product Recall*, Business Horizons, 42(2), 69-78.

Borah, A., Tellis G. J., 2016, *Halo (Spillover) Effects in Social Media: Do Product Recalls of One Brand Hurt or Help Rival Brands?*, Journal of Marketing Research, 53 (2), 143-160.

Brown, J.D., *Effect of a Health Hazard Scare on Consumer Demand*, American Journal of Agricultural Economics 51(1969):676–78.

Buzby, J. C. (2001). *Effects of food safety perceptions on food de- mand and global trade.* In A. Regmi (Ed.), Changing Structure of Global Food Consumption and Trade (pp. 55–66). Washing- ton, DC: U.S. Department of Agriculture (USDA), Economic Research Service.

Cane P., 2018, Do food recalls have a greater effect on consumers' trust when they involve healthy, organic and protected designation of origin foods and, if yes, why?, Journal of Agronomy, Technology and Engineering Management, Vol. 1(1): 99-109

Carroll, C. (2009, February). Defying a Reputational Crisis - Cadbury's Salmonella Scare: Why are Customers Willing to Forgive and Forget? Retrieved from https://www.researchgate.net/publication/240232926.

Chen, Y., Ganesan, S., Liu, Y., 2009, *Does a firm's product recall strategy affect its financial value? An examination of strategic alternatives during product-harm crises,* Journal of Marketing 73 (6), 214–226.

Cincotta, K. (2005, October 31). Less fluff more facts, industry learns. B&T: News. Retrieved May 8, 2006, from http://www.bandt.com.au/news/bd/0c037bbd.asp. Week US. Retrieved March 7, 2009, from http://www.prweekus.com/

Cleeren K., Van Heerde H. J., Dekimpe M. G., 2013, Rising from the Asches: How brands and Catergories can overcome Product harm crises, Volume 77 (March 2013), 58–77

Coombs T., 2014, The value of communication during a crisis: Insights from strategic communication research, Business Horizons.

Coombs T., Information and compassion in crisis responses: a test of their effects, Journal of public relations reaserch, 11(2), 125- 142, 1999.

Coombs, T., 2007, *Protecting organization reputations during a crisis: the development and application of situational crisis communication theory.* Corporate Reputation Review, 10(3), 163-176. http://dx.doi. org/10.1057/palgrave.crr.1550049.

Coombs, T., Holladay S.J., 2009, *Further explorations of post-crisis communication: Effects of media and response strategies on perceptions and intentions,* Public relations Review, Volume 35, 1-6.

Costello, S. P.,. Furfari K. A, 2015, "The Product Crisis: Staying Ahead by Planning Ahead," (accessed December 6, 2016), [available at http://www.jonesday.com/files/Publication/947ad59b-9bc8-4226-b4e3-013fd94f6dd7/Presentation/PublicationAttachment/de02e287-540a-4fd1-9fcd-0e9072bd66a1/TheProductCrisis.pdf].

Craig S. N., Thomas R. J., 1996, *A strategic approach to managing product recalls*, Harvard Business Review 74 (5), 102–112.

Davidson, W., Worrell D., 1992, *The Effect of Product Recall Announcements on Shareholder Wealth*, Strategic Management Journal, 13 (6), 467–73.

Dawar, N., Pillutla, M., 2000, *Impact of Product- Harm Crises on Brand Equity: The Moderating Role of Consumer Expectations*, Journal of Marketing Research, 37 (May), 215–26.

Dawes, R. M. (1979). The robust beauty of improper linear models in decision-making. American Psychologist, 34(7), 571 – 582.

De Jonge, J., H. van Trijp, J. R. Renes, and L. J. Frewer, 2007. *Understanding consumer confidence in the safety of food: its two-dimensional structure and determinants.* Risk Anal. 27(3): 729–740.

De Alessi, L., Staaf, R. J. (1994). *What does reputation really assure? The relationship of trademarks to expectations and legal remedies.* Economic Inquiry, 32, 477–485.

Eccles, R., Newquist, S., Schatz, R., 2007, *Reputation and its risks.* Harvard business review. 85. 104-14, 156.

Eilert M., Jayachandran S., Kalaignanam K., Swartz T. A., 2017. Does it pay to recall your product early? an empirical investigation in the automobile industry. Journal of Marketing 81 (3), 111–129.

Eisenhower, D., 1957, "A speech to the National Defense Executive Reserve Conference in Washington, D.C., November 14, 1957", in: D. Eisenhower, Public Papers of the Presidents of the United States, National Archives and Records Service, Government Printing Office, p. 818.

Elliot C., 2009, A Cold Cut Crisis: Listeriosis, Maple Leaf Foods, and the Politics of Apology, Canadian Journal of Communication, Vol 34 (2009) 189-204

European Food Safety Authority. 2011, *Urgent advice on the public health risk of*

*Shiga-toxin producing Escherichia coli in fresh vegetables.* EFSA J. 9(6):2274–2324.

Fearn-Banks, K., 2001, *Crisis communications: A casebook approach* (2nd ed.). Mahwah, NJ: Lawrence Erlbaum.

Fearn-Banks, K., 2007, *Crisis communication: A casebook approach. Mahwah,* NJ: Lawrence Erlbaum Associates.

Gao H., Xie J., Wang Q., Wilbur K. C., 2015. *Should ad spending increase or decrease before a recall announcement? the marketing–finance interface in product-harm crisis management,* Journal of Marketing 79 (5), 80–99.

Garcia Contreras A. F., Ceberio M., Kreinovich V., 2017, *Plans Are Worthless but Planning Is Everything: A Theoretical Explanation of Eisenhower's Observation,* Departmental Technical Reports (CS). 1102. http://digitalcommons.utep.edu/cs_techrep/1102.

Govindaraj S., Jaggi B., Lin B., 2004, *Market overreaction to product recall revisited—the case of firestone tires and the ford explorer,* Review of Quantitative Finance and Accounting 23 (1), 31–54.

Hammel M., Yamada Y, Canniatti Ponchio M., Almeida Cordeiro R., Iara Strehlau V., 2016, *The Influence Of Product Recall On Consumer Loyalty Influência Do Recall De Produtos Sobre A Lealdade Do Consumidor* Revista de Administração da UNIMEP. v.14, n.1, Janeiro/Abril

Hogarth, R. M. (1980). Judgement and choice. New York: Wiley.

Howell G.V.J., Miller R., 2010 *Maple Leaf Foods: Crisis and containment case study,* Public Communication Review, Vol. 1.

Johansson F., Brynielsson J., 2012, *Estimating Citizen Alertness in Crises using Social Media Monitoring and Analysis,* 2012 European Intelligence and Security Informatics Conference

Kalaignanam, K., Kushwaha, T., Eilert, M., 2013. The impact of product recalls on future product reliability and future accidents: Evidence from the automobile industry. Journal of Marketing 77 (2), 41–57.

Klein, N. M. (1983). Utility and decision strategies: A second look at the rational decision maker. Organizational Behavior and

Human Performance, 31(1), 1–25.

Kleinmuntz, B. (1990). Why we still use our heads instead of formulas? Toward an integrative approach. Psychological Bulletin, 107(3), 296–310.

Knight J., 1982, *Tylenol's Maker Shows How to Respond to Crisis,*

https://www.washingtonpost.com/archive/business/1982/10/11/tylenols-maker-shows-how-to-respond-to-crisis/bc8df898-3fcf-443f-bc2f-e6fbd639a5a3/ (accessed Sept 2019).

Krystek, U. (1987). Description, prevention and management of survival critical processes in companies, (First Edition). Gabler, Wiesbaden.

Kumar, S. and Budin, E.M. (2006). Prevention and Management of product recalls in the processed food industry: a case study based on an exporter's perspective. Technovation, 26(5), pp.739-750.

Laufer, D., Coombs T., 2006, *"How Should a Company Respond to a Product Harm Crisis? The Role of Corporate Reputation and Consumer-Based Cues,* Business Horizons, 49 (5), 379–85.

Magno, F.; Cassia, F.; Marino, A., 2010, Exploring customers' reaction to product recall messages: the role of responsability, opportunism and brand reputation. In: Global Conference On Business & Economics, 10, Roma.

Magno, F., 2012, *Managing product recalls: the effects of time, responsible vs. opportunistic recall management and blame on consumers' attitudes.* Procedia Social and Behavioral Sciences, v. 58, p. 1309–1315.

Moore, T., 1982, The fight to save Tylenol, Fortune, October 7

Mowen, J. C., 1980, *Further information on consumer percep- tions of product recalls.* Advances in Consumer Research, 7(1), 519–523.

Mowen, J. C., Jolly, D.; Nickell, G. S., 1981, Factors influencing consumer responses to product recalls: a regression analysis approach. Advances in Consumer Research, v. 8, p. 405–407.

MSNBC.COM. (2010). Toyota recall timeline. Retrieved from http://www.msnbc.msn.com/id/35240466/ns/business-autos/. Accessed April 27, 2011.

Mukherjee A., Chauhan S., 2019, *The Impact of Product Recall on Advertising Decisions and Firm Profit While Envisioning Crisis or Being Hazard Myopic* CIRRELT-2019-16, April.

Owles, Eric and McDermon, Daniel. (2010). A Toyota timeline. nytimes.com, February 10, 2010. Retrieved from

http://www.nytimes.com/interactive/2010/02/10/business/20100210_TOYOTA_TI MELI NE2.html. Accessed April 27, 2011.

Rhee M., Haunschild P. R., 2006, "The Liability of Good Reputation," Organization Science, 17 (1), 101–117.

Rohini A. , Burnkrant R. E., Unnava, H.R., 2000, "Consumer Response to Negative Publicity: The Moderating Role of Commitment," Journal of Marketing Research, 37 (May), 203–214.

Roth G., 1992, Field Marshal von Moltke the Elder His Importance Then and Now, Army History, PB-20-92-3 (No. 23) Washington D.C.

Shrivastava P., Mitroff I., Miller D., Miglani A., 1988, Understanding industrial crisis, Journal of Management studies, 25:4, July, 287-303

Siomkos, G. J., 1989, *Managing product-harm crisis. Industrial Crisis Quartely,* v. 3, n. 1, p. 41–60.

Siomkos, G. J. *On achieving exoneration after a product safety industrial crisis.* Journal of Business & Industrial Marketing, v. 14, p. 17–19, 1999. J. of the Acad. Mark. Sci

Siomkos, G. J.; Kurzbard, G., 1992, *Crafting a damage control plan, a lesson from Perrier,* The Journal of Business Strategy, March April, 39-43.

Siomkos, G. and Shrivastava, P., 1993, *Responding to Product Liability Crises. Long Range Planning,* 26(5), pp.72-79.

Siomkos, G. J.; Kurzbard, G. 1994, *The hidden crisis in product-harm crisis management.* European Journal of Marketing, v. 28, n. 2, p. 30–41.

Tajitsu N., *Japanese airbag maker Takata files for bankruptcy, gets Chinese backing,* Reuters, 2017, https://www.reuters.com/article/us-takata-bankruptcy-japan/japanese-airbag-maker-takata-files-for-bankruptcy-gets-chinese-backing-idUSKBN19G0Z [Online; accessed 11-October-2019].

United States Department of Justice Criminal Division Fraud Section, Year 2016, 2017.

Van Heerde, H., Helsen K., Dekimpe M. 2007, *The Impact of a Product-Harm Crisis on Marketing Effectiveness,* Marketing Science, 26 (2), 230–45.

Venette S. J., 2003, *Risk communication in a High Reliability Organisation: APHIS PPQ's inclusion of risk in decision making,* MI: UMI Proquest Information and Learning.

Verbeke, W., Ward R.W., and Viaene J., 2000, *Probit Analysis of Fresh Meat Consumption in Belgium: Exploring BSE and Television Communication Impact,* Agribusiness. 16:215-234.

Von Moltke, *1995,* On the art of war: selected writings, Daniel Hugens Editor.

Wimmer E., 2012, Toyota: An Auto Giant Overcoming a Gigantic Crisis In: Motoring the Future. Palgrave Macmillan, London

World Health Organization. 22 July 2011. Outbreaks of E. coli O104:H4 infection:

update 30. Available at: http://www.euro.who.int/en/what-we-do/health-topics/emergencies/international-health-regulations/news/news/2011/07/outbreaks-of-e.-coli-o104h4-infection-update-30. Accessed 18 October 2011.

# ABOUT THE AUTHOR

Paola Cane is a senior advisor and author, expert in compliance issues, product recalls and product harm crises. Her extensive experience includes preventing, detecting and responding to varied product hazards in the food, pharmaceutical, cosmetics and feed sector. She has traveled and lectured internationally providing best practice guidance for recall response and crisis management. This is her third book.

Printed in Great Britain
by Amazon